New Moon
Over
Slick Rock Hollow

*Notes in the Life of a
Mountain Preacher's Wife*

by Martha Stoltzfus

Copyright © 2005
by
Martha Stoltzfus
4227 Bowlings Creek
Jackson, KY 41339

Library of Congress Control Number: 2005927563
International Standard Book Number: 1-932864-27-x

Printed by
Masthof Press
219 Mill Road
Morgantown, PA 19543-9516

Dedication

Dedicated to the memory

of my beloved husband,

Wesley Stoltzfus.

He was given to me "to have and to hold,"

for nearly fifty years.

Now he has been taken away . . . for a season.

We will meet again.

Table of Contents

Chapter 1:	New Moon 1

Chapter 2:	The End of the Road 7

Chapter 3:	God's Surprises 17
~ The Power of the Word
~ Shattered Dreams
~ Even Babies Shall Hear
~ Bethel on the Greyhound Bus
~ Screwdriver Angel

Chapter 4:	Bind Up the Brokenhearted 28
~ The Wake
~ Jesus Has a Rocking Chair
~ Good Old Country Boy

Chapter 5:	The Way It Was 35
~ Across the Hills and Down the Hollers
by Will Johnson
~ Mommy the Matriarch
by Mose Turner
~ I'm Proud of My Heritage
by Willie Johnson
~ Seasons of Home
by Woodrow Deaton
~ Mother's Helper
by Elsie Raleigh Johnson
~ Feb Fork of Gays Creek
by Wesley Stoltzfus

Chapter 6:   Christmas in the Hills 79

Chapter 7:   Mother's Day for Sally 94

Chapter 8:   Heart Notes 97
              ~ An Ode of Praise for My Fingers
              ~ Touch the Moment
              ~ A Snake Hike
              ~ Lizards and Coffins
              ~ Mom's Hands—A Eulogy
              ~ Sunday Stroll

Chapter 9:   Flight—The Empty Nest 105

Chapter 10:   Bowlings Creek Mennonite Church 132
              ~ Bowlings Creek Reflections
                by Wesley Stoltzfus
              ~ Introducing Our Church
              ~ Mama and the Preacher
              ~ Fire at the Church
              ~ The Flower Bed Story

Chapter 11:   Decision Time 153

Chapter 12:   Room 400. 155

Chapter 13:   Twilight, the Beginning. 164

Chapter 14:   He Bottles Our Tears 177

Introduction

It doesn't take long to live a life, yet myriads of experiences combine to form that life. This book is simply a collection of a few of those experiences, especially as they relate to life in the Hills of Eastern Kentucky as a preacher's wife. Some pages were written years before Wesley's death. Others more recently.

Several years after *Hope in the Deepest Hollow* was published, my pastor husband, Wesley, went Home to be with the Lord. Shortly before his death in 2003, he said to me, "After my death, I hope you can write again." My reaction was, *No! I'll never be able to write again.* Since that time there has been sufficient healing so I can say "yes" to Wesley's request and "yes" to my Lord when he nudges me to pick up my pen and write.

These pages are also written in response to many friends who encouraged me by asking, "When are you going to write another book?" The positive response and affirmation from you, the readers of my first book, has been overwhelming. Thanks for your encouragement.

Thank you, Fern, for helping me again. You are a special daughter. Thanks for your valuable suggestions and practical help. You spent countless hours editing and arranging my jumbled pages, and correcting my grammar and punctuation. Mose Turner, you can be proud of Fern; she learned well in your classroom.

Several good friends shared some of their life experiences with me and agreed to let you also read them. Thanks to Will Johnson, Mose and Eva Turner, Willie Johnson, Woodrow Deaton, and Elsie Raleigh Johnson.

– CHAPTER 1 –

New Moon

The morning mist was lifting, exposing the distant green hills inch by inch. Soon the sun would burn it all away, even the heavy fog over the river. The waning sliver of moon had just set in the West and the spring air was chilly. Quiet. Peaceful. Beautiful. I would never tire of this early morning scene from our deck at Slick Rock Hollow.

But then, uneasy thoughts drifted into my quiet mind. Several weeks earlier Steve Swartz had called Wesley. "I'm helping Sunrise Chapel near Fort Wayne, Indiana, find an interim pastor. Would you consider that assignment?"

I assumed the answer would be an immediate "No." And, without any prayers or discussion, that would be the end. Instead, Wesley began now and again to talk about this thing. I was thinking, *Please, let's not even talk about it. There's no way we will leave Kentucky to go to Indiana. We are too old. Wesley's health is sporadic. We are enjoying fewer responsibilities in the church. Our life here together is settled, predictable, retired, and comparatively easy. We would miss our people and our place. I'm a homebody. Please, can't we just stay at home? And, dear friend, Belle—who would see about her? She has nobody else.*

More recently, Wesley and I had begun to discuss the possibility. "This invitation just won't go away," he said. "We can't say no until we make it a definite matter of prayer and discern the mind of the Lord in this matter."

That morning on our dew-drenched deck, my Lord and I had a long talk. The basic question He asked, "Are you willing to leave the comforts of home and go with your husband to Fort Wayne, Indiana?"

I finally said, "I'm willing to be made willing." The Lord took it from there. I began to search the scriptures to find what God wants us to do and how will we know? I found the question is not **How** does God lead? But, do you believe He **will** lead? Can you trust Him to be there when you don't see the **how**? And, will you follow?

*He who has compassion on them **will guide them** and lead them beside springs of water.* (Isaiah 49:10)

I will instruct you and teach you in the way you should go. (Psalm 32:8)

The Lord will watch over your coming and going, from this time forth and even forever. (Psalm 121:8)

And, of course, the promise in James 1:5 that I have claimed countless times: *If any of you lacks wisdom, he should ask God who **gives generously** to all, without scolding.*

One day I read God's promise to Jacob and I decided it was God's promise to us also. *I am with you and will watch over you wherever you go, and **I will bring you back to this land**. I will not leave you until I have done what I have promised you.*

The Lord gently led this reluctant and fearful servant to the place where I could say, "I'm ready to go—but let's not stay very long." Gradually that attitude changed to an expectant eagerness to follow Jesus and to follow Wesley no matter how long or where.

The moon was coming in again, when together we agreed to call Steve. "We are available." We made arrangements with the mailman and the garbage man and did some preliminary packing. The church people honored us with a farewell dinner, and many hugs and, "Do you have to leave?" words. Then came the delays. Housing for us at Sunrise Chapel wasn't complete. Then Wesley developed a mysterious allergy and was hospitalized several days. Later he had a bad infection on his leg.

New Moon Over Slick Rock Hollow

Our decision to go to Indiana was tested. "We don't know what's going on, Lord, but we know you are in control and we know you are leading us, so we rest."

A new moon rose and a full moon set another time. Finally the call came from Joe at Sunrise Chapel. "We are ready here when you are."

Early on a May morning in 2002 we loaded our Buick, disconnected the water heater and refrigerator, adjusted the furnace thermostat, locked the doors and headed North. Expectations were high. Adrenalin was working overtime. Wesley's ministry at Sunrise Chapel would be rewarding, I assured him. This would be a blessed interval in our lives.

I was totally unprepared for the next two months of homesickness and depression. There was a heaviness, a deep sadness, and loneliness. I cried much for no apparent reason. During the first church service at Sunrise Chapel I cried through the whole meeting. Our children came to see us, or called us, and I cried when they left. I couldn't pray very long because I just broke down and cried.

Guilt plagued me. *It's a sin to feel sorry for yourself. You have everything you need. The church people are extremely good to you; they provided you with a beautiful trailer home, completely furnished, rent free. They bring flowers and food and encouragement. You aren't being persecuted. You don't have a terminal illness. You and Wesley have each other. So, Smile! Sing! Shout! Praise the Lord!*

The sadness continued. Wesley was fighting the same battle, but his guilt feelings took a different turn. *Here I sit, doing nothing, and the church is paying me a salary. It isn't right.* He slept much, and was extremely exhausted. I recalled the question the Israelites put to Moses, "Why did you bring us here, to die in this **wilderness**?" We postponed bedtime because we dreaded the next day. The full moon shone on our bed and I cried, "How many months must I endure this?" I struggled to keep my mind from negative thoughts and my eyes from tears, but soon I was tasting salt again.

Within this emotional upheaval, I refused to allow it to invade my spirit. Again and again I told the Lord I didn't understand, but I trusted Him to continue to perfect His work in us. I begged Him to clothe me with a garment of praise instead of this spirit of heaviness, and to please let me go back home.

One morning when I awoke, I discovered the gloom was lifted! I felt good emotionally. I praised God again and again. But, by evening, discouragement returned. Not overnight but, gradually, the Lord replaced the heavy negative feelings with hope and joy. The darkness was gone and I was able to enjoy life again.

"Partly cloudy," the Fort Wayne area weatherman had predicted. He was partly right, but the sky was so much more. Without hills to obscure the view, the sky was large and bright with constantly changing cloud patterns. All that was only a prelude for the sunset. I placed my lawn chair behind our trailer to wait and watch and worship. For a full hour and more I watched my Creator paint a panorama of color over half the sky. It was absolutely awesome! It seemed my Lord was saying, "I know you miss the beauty of Bowlings Creek. See, northern Indiana is beautiful also." I was moved to tears and I worshipped.

In all that splendor, I kept looking for the new moon. To me, a new moon signals a new beginning. Troubles come and troubles go, but there is always a New Moon. I had checked the calendar and knew about when and where to expect the moon's location. Darkness was moving in and there was Venus, large and bright. Still the sunset colors moved and brightened. I scanned the western sky for the new moon. It was getting darker and suddenly, I saw it! Hanging close to the western horizon, between Venus and the fading sunset. I wept. "Lord, you are in northern Indiana as surely as in eastern Kentucky. No matter where on this earth I find myself, the moon will be there. No matter where or what this life holds, you, Lord are there!"

New Moon Over Slick Rock Hollow

Day is dying in the West,
Heaven is touching earth with rest.
Wait and worship while the night
Sets her evening lamps alight, through all the sky.
Holy! Holy! Holy! Lord God of Hosts!

This rather scary experience of a period of despondency; I don't want it wasted, so I ponder the lessons learned:

~ I know that emotional illness and instability is as serious a sickness as heart disease, and just as frustrating. I know God cares.

~ I have a lot more empathy for other women who suffer from homesickness. I think of the pioneer women who left their homes and friends and parents, to go "West" with their husbands, never expecting to see Home again. I think of today's pioneer women, leaving their parental home place, moving from east to west, or north to south to follow their husband and his career. And I think of our daughters, miles from home and eventually building homes elsewhere. And I wonder how many tears were shed and how many prayers were prayed.

~ Was some of the gloom I experienced from Satan? I don't know. I simply told the Lord, "If this is an attack from your enemy, I reject it. If it is a disciplinary measure from you, I receive it and rejoice."

~ I suspect the Lord is trying to wean me from depending on the comforts of home, the security of things and the luxury of retirement. Instead, to trust Him for my security and comfort.

~ I give up the right to know **why** God does what He does in my life. Sometimes He shows us; often He doesn't.

~ My Father is closely monitoring my growth. "Every branch that bears fruit, He prunes it so it will bear more fruit."

~ I'm so glad our emotions are not a true indicator of our relationship with our God.

There will always be another New Moon.

Slick Rock Hollow plunging into Bowlings Creek.

– CHAPTER 2 –

The End of the Road

"Where do you live?"

When people ask, we usually say, "At the end of the road. Just follow 1110 from Haddix, 20 miles, to Turner Grocery at the Head of Bowlings Creek. Drive down the creek, curve around the hill several miles, past the church, and you better slow down some more because the blacktop road ends here. But, keep going, you aren't there yet. Another mile and the road narrows to barely one lane. Don't worry; you probably won't meet any oncoming traffic. When you think *surely nobody lives way down here*, there it is—the End of the Road and our place, Slick Rock Hollow."

Some people, when they find us, say, "How did you ever find this God-forsaken place?"

Others say, "I'd give anything to live at a secluded place like this. It's so peaceful."

For 35 years we had been a preacher's family, living in the parsonage just several feet from the church house. Since it was church property, it was rent free and very convenient. We were free to raise our large family there even though they put a hole in the wall with a basketball, and wore out several linoleum rugs in the kitchen, and were guilty of other minor misdemeanors and acts of vandalism. It was convenient because the preacher could also be the janitor and maintenance man for the church property. And the preacher's wife could be hostess to evangelists and other visitors to the church.

It was convenient, but it was called "Wesley's church." Wesley felt very uncomfortable with that image. "This is not Wesley's church. It is The Lord's church. I don't own the church; it belongs to Jesus. Responsibility—yes. Ownership—no. I must keep my grubby hands off what belongs to God." In that context, we began to pray and consider the possibility of putting distance between the preacher and the church building.

Besides, it would be nice to have a place of our own, to have a deed for a piece of God's earth. The church house and parsonage are all church property; it belongs to Rosedale Mennonite Missions. We also looked ahead to our retirement time when we would no doubt be replaced by another pastor for the church. To have our own house would be a blessing. However, there was no way we could buy any property on our income. We had no bank account to speak of and no savings. But the Lord turned that impossibility into a possible situation.

One day, back in the 1980s, the phone rang. It was Mom Stoltzfus.

"Wesley, would you consider moving back to Lancaster County, Pennsylvania, to farm? I'm consulting all my children. If no one wants to take on our farm, I'm ready to sell it." Several years earlier, Wesley's father had passed away. His brother Mark had farmed some, but now there would be a change; Mom was selling the home farm. Wesley did consider, we prayed, and soon called Mom back.

"The answer is 'no,' Mom. You know I'm not a dairy farmer. I would be no good for the place; it would go to pot and the cows would stop giving milk. Besides, my ministry is right here and I sense no leading to leave Kentucky."

So Rohrers Hill Farm was sold at a public auction. It was a sad day for all the Dan A. Stoltzfus family. Years and years of family life ended when the auctioneer shouted, "Going, going, gone!" A local Amish man bought it and he soon disconnected the electricity and removed all electric light fixtures to accommodate the Amish lifestyle for him and his growing family.

After the farm was sold and the estate settled, at each year's end, Mom sent to each of her seven children several thousand dollars, to avoid paying the huge property tax. For us, those end of year bonuses were very welcome. We used them to pay our taxes and to buy old klonkers of cars.

Wesley made a decision, "We've got to stop using up all our inheritance money on cars. From now on we'll put that money in savings 'til we can buy some property of our own."

However, finding available and affordable property on Bowlings Creek or the surrounding area was another impossibility. There were many empty houses and abandoned hillside farms, but they weren't for sale; many were tied up in heir's ownership and couldn't be touched. So, even if we had the money, there was absolutely no appropriate real estate available. That's what we thought.

After Mother Stoltzfus' death, Wesley came home one day and announced, "I learned that A.B. and Janice want to sell their property just below Levi's place. It's part of the original Rob Combs farm." I got excited! On June 7, 1982, Wesley and I went to the lawyer's office in Jackson and signed the papers that transferred the property into our name, "to have and to hold the same." Now I was really excited!

I calmed down somewhat when I realized all the planning and hard work that faced us. We had bought a plot of several acres, much of which was steep unusable hillside. (The deed stated: two acres, more or less. "More" meaning hillside, I guess.) The rest sloped gradually to the creek bottom. There were no buildings, just 15 years growth of brush and saplings and weeds overall. But we saw the possibilities and we went to work. We bushhogged (Wait! Save the Dogwood trees! And the Redbud!) and planted and built. Wesley and I spent hours designing the house. Dave and Dan planted an orchard, counting on their expertise from studying at Morehead State University's Ag program.

I spent hours planning flower beds and borders. One day I crossed the creek and walked up the hollow and over the hill to Curly Head and Mandy's old homestead. I carried a trowel and a sack. Nothing is left of their home but a chimney and rows of Easter flags. Mandy had planted them many years ago. Very carefully, I dug some bulbs for my own homestead. "Mandy," I said, "thanks for the Easter flags. I knew you wouldn't mind if I got some."

Except for rock walls, Wesley thinks landscaping is very optional. Through the years, whether or not to plant a tree or a bush or flowers has been one of our bases for quarrels. The way we quarrel is this: He says, "This stuff (bushes, flowers, whatever) just makes more work for you! You're already working too hard in the hot sun. Besides, that tree is in the way. When I get on my mower, I want to mow, not look out for all those saplings and bushes. And those pine needles get all down my back!" I just let him fuss, and then I wait to catch him gone, and plant another tree! I have adopted Uncle John Blank's motto: "Plant until you are planted."

Seven of our nine children were gone from home when we bought the property, but they all helped to build. They mixed mud, dug footer, laid block, cut timber, hammered, and painted. They brought their spouses and friends to help. It was truly a family project.

When we finally moved into our new home on October 11, 1986, we knew without a doubt, this is a gift from our Lord. How else can you explain it? There was seemingly no property available, and we had no money. At that time the land and the house was all paid for. Father loves to give his young'uns good things to enjoy! In this miracle He used inheritance money.

* * * *

On that eventful October day, we were moving from the parsonage to Slick Rock Hollow. It was time for Wesley and Martha's children to close the door of their childhood home. Their safe and secluded haven was being dismembered box by box. But it was time to move on. Rosie spoke for all of them when she said, "It's sad, Mom, but we all are so glad you and Dad can have this new place at the end of the road."

That Saturday night, with unpacked boxes stacked shoulder high in every room, Wesley called Lisa and Carol and me into the new kitchen. We joined hands. He dedicated this place to God and to His work. "It's yours, Lord, not ours. We thank you that you let us enjoy and use it. Do with us and this place whatever you want." Then he added, "And, Lord, tell Dad and Mom 'thanks' for all the hard work they put into that farm so we can enjoy this new house."

Later, when I lay down on my bed, feeling just a trifle insecure in unfamiliar surroundings, I heard the familiar creak of Wesley's swivel chair in the study room across the hall. He was preparing his sermon for the next morning. I felt snug and went to sleep.

* * * *

What's in a name? When it comes to names of hollows, I often wonder about their origin. There are hundreds of hollows and side roads and creeks in Eastern Kentucky, and most have a name. Some are self-explanatory: Deaton Branch, Silas Road, and Mud Hole Holler. Others are more mysterious: Horse Holler, Rock House Hollow, Lick Branch, Bushes Branch, Cow Creek, Canoe Fork, Squabble Creek, and Rowdy. Over on Grapevine there is a Noodle Creek and a Copperhead Bend. There is a hollow across from the church house. When we lived there I would sometimes walk up that hollow to briefly escape the noisy heat of a summer family. Except for the church basement, it was the only cool place around. I don't think it has a name, but if I could, I would name it Cool Creek or Shady Solitude.

The deed to our property that we bought from A.B. and Janice, describes it in part as follows, to-wit, "Beginning at a

The house that Wesley built at the end of the road.

sycamore tree at the mouth of the **Slick Rock Hollow**, running up the creek to the next hollow by a thorn tree, thence running straight up the hollow to the top of the hill by an oak . . ."

    In the wintertime I can see Slick Rock Hollow from our living room window, the stream falling over rocks down to the creek. In summer it's a shaded, mostly dry narrow chasm. I am intrigued with the name. No doubt there was once a slick rock. Is it still there? Years ago, Flory Stamper walked the creek every morning and evening to school. She knows the hollow, but she remembers nothing about a slick rock, or why the name.

It seemed natural to call this homestead Slick Rock Hollow. We thought of other names: WesMar (Wesley and Martha), Dogwood Drive, and Cedar Cliffs. But Slick Rock Hollow fits. It sounds country and homey. Rosie says to her family, "Let's go down to Slick Rock Hollow to see Mom and Dad."

When Steve calls, he says "Hi, Mom. How are things at Slick Rock?" And to our Briar Hoppin' grandchildren, "Kentucky" and "Papaw and Mamaw's Place" and "Slick Rock Hollow" are synonymous.

Rohrers Hill Farm Memories

In the summer of 1999, a group of the Dan A. Stoltzfus *"friendshaft"* (extended family), including Wesley's family, made an ancestral trip to various family historical points of interest. One of those places was The Home Farm, officially called Rohrers Hill Farm, which had been out of the family for many years.

"We will not be at home that day. Please be free to go all through the house and barn and farm. We won't mind." The current owners of the place were very generous. The Stoltzfus family accepted their invitation. What memories! What emotions! Everybody went all through the large two-story brick farmhouse, remembering. Wesley began to reminisce about his boyhood days on this farm.

"This little room back here—we called it the Bill Evans kich because Bill was one of many homeless people who worked for Dad. (That room is also where Wesley was born.) And down here in the basement were the huge iron kettles where Mom made gallons of potato chips and many pounds of lye soap and where she blanched bushels of sweet corn for the freezer. I remember the big dinner bell that was in that belfry on the roof. The rope hung right here and we pulled it only for dinner or for emergencies. Here is the pantry. I remember Mom's molasses cookies. When she baked, she made enough to fill a lard can full. When I came home from school and got ready to do the barn chores, I stuffed my pockets with molasses cookies. They were hard and chewy, so I would soak them in the water running from the pipe to the cattle's water tank, out by the barn."

Wesley also relished his Mother's shoofly pies. We found this note stuck in Grusmommy's cookbook, right beside the shoofly pie recipe.

Dear Mother,
My teeth into this pie I've sunk,
Twas on the way up to my bunk.
I've eaten quite a bit, you see,
And really, they taste good to me.
(No bunk.)
Thanks!! . . . . . . Wes (May 4, 1954)

Wesley rambled all through the barn. The cow stable looked much the same. "Each cow was tied to her place to be milked. Here is where what's-her-name stood. How could I forget her name? She was a mean kicker. Nobody but Mom could milk her; she just had a way with mean cows. Here was the horse barn. When we kids were young, Dad farmed with mules and horses, but he couldn't afford sound critters. One horse was a cribber, constantly chewing on her feed crib. One pair of mules had spent years in a stone quarry and their toes were permanently damaged. They always walked on their toes. No blacksmith could help them. But they were fast and pulled hard. Once Dad bought a horse that was constantly urinating, and she was mean. If she took a notion, at the end of the row, instead of turning around, she backed. Pity the kid riding the tobacco planter behind her!"

Swinging bridge over the middle fork of the Kentucky River.

"And here is the ladder to the hay mow. I remember if it was a rainy day, I would come up here and sleep. When I heard the weather vane creaking, I knew the wind was changing, the rain would soon stop and we would have to get back to working the fields."

Next he went to check out the spring house. Inside was a spring of water, bubbling up and running over flat rocks. It was always a cool place.

"Years ago the springhouse was used for a milk cooler. A local blacksmith made a cart for Dad. It was custom-designed with two buggy wheels and was equipped to hold three or four ten-gallon milk cans. After each morning and evening milking of 20-25 cows, the milk was strained into those huge milk cans and wheeled down to the springhouse. There we submerged the cans into the cold spring water. Each morning the milk man arrived and hauled the cold milk to a milk processing plant. The springhouse was also used as a refrigerator. A watermelon never tasted any better than when it was brought into the yard from the spring, dripping wet and cold."

"My Dad loved to eat mackerel fish. He would buy a wooden bucket full of mackerel preserved in a salty brine. When Mom planned to fix some for breakfast, she would remove some fish from the bucket and place it in the spring water over night, to soak out the salt. Then we enjoyed it with hot milk and butter over toast."

That day at the farm, memories were running free, some sad, some funny. When it was time to leave, there was time for just one more story.

"Both Dad and Mom had a fascination for Canadian geese. The majestic beauty and interesting migrating habits of these wild birds of the North Country made them very attractive. It was an exciting day on the farm when the pair of geese arrived that Dad had bought from somebody out towards the Bay. I don't know what he paid for them, but I'm sure they didn't come cheap. He intended to clip their wings until they were acclimated to the farm and then put them on our farm pond. They were a mated pair so perhaps they would raise some young and we would have lots of Canadian Geese. We kids all gathered around the crate and admired the beautiful birds. Dad had fixed a small temporary pen for the geese and everything was ready. He opened the crate and very carefully lifted out the gander, clipped his wings and placed him in the pen. Then he picked up the goose by her wings. At that instant she tried to wrench free, fell over on her back and died. Nobody spoke; we were horrified! Dad just stood there a moment, then walked away, totally frustrated. 'Marian and Anna,' he said, 'pluck the goose and put her in the freezer.' The girls carried it to the house, crying all the way, but we never ate the goose. Every spring after that, for years, the gander paced back and forth at the edge of the pond, lifted his long neck and beautiful head to the sky and called his mate, 'Honk! Honk! . . . Honk! Honk!' I never forgot that lonesome sound, 'Honk! Honk!'

– CHAPTER 3 –

God's Surprises

The Power of the Word

The rag weeds were hanging onto the dusty road, heavy with enough pollen to make sneezers of those who never sneeze. Joe Pie and Iron Weed were in full bloom and dead leaves were already falling. Roscoe fenced off his cattle by the creek and mowed the pasture by the road. It was again time for the annual meetin' at Roscoe Noble's place.

The congregation of about fifty gathered in the pasture on the second Sunday in September, rain or shine. This time it was rain. We huddled under the single funeral tent and listened to the preacher. Rain dripped from the tent top onto his back, and he preached on. Someone held an umbrella over the other preachers waiting in line to preach, and he preached on. When the rain stopped, the preacher was energized anew, so he kept on preaching and singing. With long strides and loud voice he proclaimed the salvation of our God. Young boys scrambled to pick up the paper paraphernalia that fell out of his Bible when he waved it over his head.

Even though we prayed for the rain to stop, I thought the falling rain was appropriate. *The rain comes down and waters the earth, to produce seed and grain so we can LIVE* (Isaiah 55). The message of God is rained on receptive hearts, to produce LIFE. When it was Wesley's turn to preach, he illustrated that truth as he told of Floyd Noble's spiritual journey.

"When I first knew Floyd he was rather antagonistic about Christ and the Church. An evangelist and I went to see him one day. We reminded him that he needed to be saved. 'I am one of those born to be lost,' he informed us. I think what he was really saying was, 'Get off my back, preacher.'" I did, for a while. After his wife, Lillie Belle, died, he was lonely. When I next visited him he was reading a small New Testament."

"I see you are reading the Bible."

"Yes. I've read this little book through many times since Lillie Belle died."

"What are you reading?" I asked him. He told me what he was reading and I sensed enlightenment and a desire for God. The Light was beginning to penetrate the darkness. The power of the Word was apparent.

"My eyes are failing and I can't see to read very well," he said. I promised to bring him a large print Bible and promptly forgot. On my next visit he reminded me of my promise, so I brought him a large print Bible and he continued to read and learn. The message of the gospel had a powerful effect on his life.

One day I said, "Floyd, you don't believe that anymore; about being born to be lost, do you?"

His face softened. "No," he said. "I don't." Soon after that he asked Roy Moore to take him to the river to baptize him. Not long after that, he died. The Lord used the witness of His people in Floyd's life, but, most importantly, He used the Power of His Word.

At our little meeting, the rain had stopped and the final preacher had preached. It was time for "Dinner on the Grounds." The food was served on long tables beside the tent. Food was kept in coolers and cookers and boxes on the back of pick-up trucks until serving time. Most women bring the best of their best to memorial meetings. They cook all day, early and late–fried chicken, ham, chicken 'n dumplings, all sorts of beans, potato salad of all descriptions, casseroles and salads, some traditional, some rather new. Desserts covered one whole table—cakes, pies, puddings, fancy cream cheese and chocolate concoctions, delights, gingerbread, apple hand pies. All this was devoured with corn bread, pop, and coffee.

We had barely circled the tables twice (or thrice) and decided we could eat no more, when it began to rain again—hard. The food was hurriedly covered and carried away. People ran for shelter.

I pray that God's message will not be preached in vain, but it will encourage people to change their plans, to run for protection from God's wrath. I pray that God's Word, as the rain, will bear fruit.

Shattered Dreams

> *If you spend yourselves in behalf of the hungry and satisfy the needs of the oppressed, then your light will rise in the darkness.*

Someone was at the door. A young man stood there. He had an unkempt appearance, a week's growth of whiskers, and drugged eyes. He hung his head, apparently ashamed for anyone to see his face, and there were several bottles of prescription medications protruding from his jacket pocket.

Wesley seated him on a kitchen chair, took his face in both his hands and looked him in the eyes. "Son, where have you been?" It was obvious that wherever he had been, the journey had been difficult and down.

We first knew him as a winsome, small child in Sunday School. Even as a child he was disadvantaged—abandoned by both parents and raised in the home of some relatives. He was a smart child and he had his dreams. "I want to go to school and learn to be a doctor." Though he had little encouragement from anywhere, he graduated from High School with good grades and went on to college on a scholarship. There he did exceptionally well, averaging a 4.0 grade point. There he was also introduced to drugs and his downhill slide began.

For the next several years he would periodically appear at our door or call us, collect. Always he was on the bottom—no money, no car or driver's license, no friends, no job, no home. His mind was distorted and his nerves shot. Always he was embarrassed and apologetic. "I started going to church and I wish I could do better, but . . . I need help. I had a bundle of clothes and a pack of cigarettes hid in a barn and somebody stole them. I need help."

Jesus came to bring deliverance to the captives. We are the hands of Jesus so we tried to help. Wesley prayed and cried with him, and gave counsel. He helped him get a bicycle so he could get to work, and gave him his personal watch so he could get there on time. He took him to a half-way place for help for his addiction. He brought him back to Jesus again. We called him Friend and Son and we loved him.

Raise the fallen, cheer the faint, heal the sick, and lead the blind. At times we gave him a bed, and several meals, and in the dead of winter when the rent was due for his empty room, we paid his rent for a month and bought him some cigarettes. I dug a quilt out of my cedar chest for him. Like Jesus, we were touched with his weaknesses. His life continued downward, in shambles and hopeless.

Now here he was again, on the bottom, asking for help. When Wesley called him "Son," he started crying. The boy has a genuine soft heart. Besides, he had just had three beers. We blessed him, and talked, and gave him a little money for cigarettes and toilet paper.

Before he left I hugged him, as I would a son. He said, "If I would have had a better chance, maybe I would have done better." He paused. "Maybe I would even be a doctor." He was gone and it was my turn to cry. *Give your shattered dreams to Jesus. Perhaps there is still time.*

Even Babies Shall Hear

It's only some tissue, they say; a choice or an irritation—this embryo growing inside a mother's womb—incapable of seeing or hearing or feeling or knowing. Really? There *is* one thing that can penetrate the walls and water of the unborn's world and causes him to respond. The preaching of the Word of God! Let me tell you this story.

We were enjoying some God-inspired meetings at a church conference in Kalona, Iowa. An attractive young mother came to me after the service. "You are Wesley's wife? Some years ago Wesley was at our church, preaching revival meetings. I was pregnant at the time with our first child. I sat at the meetings, listening. Wesley preached hard and strong. And when he preached real loud, my baby jumped! He preached some more and when he made another emphatic point, my baby jumped again, and again! After the service, I was wondering what was going on and telling my pregnant friend about my baby's 'jumps.'"

"I had the same experience!" she said. "When the preacher preached loud, my baby said, 'Amen!'"

Centuries earlier, Old Mrs. Zechariah was pregnant with her first child. The child in her womb leaped for joy when Mary, with her unborn WORD, entered the room! Elizabeth Zechariah's child became a powerful preacher of God's message of repentance. Mary's child *was* the WORD.

Whether to one unborn child, or to multitudes of people, the Word of the Lord is powerful.

Bethel on the Greyhound Bus
by Wesley

The Greyhound bus was waiting at Jackson, Kentucky. I stepped inside and found a vacant seat beside a black boy. The bus was crowded—not a spare seat anywhere—with young men on their way to Louisville, Kentucky for their physical examination, prior to being inducted into the army. I was one of them. Although I had lived in Kentucky for only several months, I was instructed to take my examination in Kentucky instead of Pennsylvania.

The bus pulled out and we were on our way. The boys began to "light up." "Want a cigarette?" my seat partner asked.

"No thanks."

The boy in front of us turned and offered me a smoke.

"No thanks."

"Here, have one," the boy across the isle generously pulled one out of his pack.

"No thanks." I repeated and looked around. Everyone was puffing on a cigarette.

We were fast rolling along, over and around those S curves and hills on the old highway, out by Slade. Suddenly I knew what motion sickness was all about. By that time the air was full of crude jokes, vile and boastful talk, and blue smoke. Without warning, my body began to desperately crave nicotine.

I had begun smoking in grade school, when I was a very young boy. Mother never allowed it in the house, but on the farm and with some friends, there were always lots of other places. By the time I entered my teens, I was addicted. Then began the long struggle to quit. For years I lived with defeat and guilt because I knew it was a bad habit. It was hindering my walk with the Lord, and I knew it would eventually kill me. It wasn't until after I had a spiritual encounter with my Lord and surrendered my spirit, soul and body to Him that I had victory over that addiction. Some can quit by sheer determination. I couldn't. God's supernatural power within me washed me from sin and from my cravings.

But now, in the hot, airless, smoky confines of that Greyhound bus, my whole body was screaming for a cigarette. Even after four years, the temptation came back. For several intense moments

I struggled. I was afraid—afraid that if I started smoking now I would never quit again.

Then I cried out to the Lord, "Lord! I need help! I don't know what to do. I'm desperate! Help me!"

Carrying a New Testament in my shirt pocket had become as much a habit as carrying my keys and pocket knife in my pants pocket. I reached into my pocket, not for a pack, but for my Bible. Before, I had not practiced opening my Bible at random for an answer, but in this desperate situation, God honored that request. I opened my Bible and the words from God in Galatians 5:1 burned themselves into my spirit. *Stand fast therefore in the liberty wherewith Christ hath made us free and be not entangled again with the yoke of bondage.*

I read it again and, suddenly, God washed that craving right out of me! It was just gone. I'll never forget the feeling of release and freedom. The power of God's Words applied to me by the Holy Spirit was awesome.

I said, "Thank you, Lord!" and tucked the New Testament back in my pocket. There on that Greyhound bus I experienced my "Bethel." God was in that place and I didn't know it. That noisy, smelly bus, full of smoke and fear? Yes! (See Genesis, chapter 28, to read about Jacob's ladder and Jacob's Bethel.)

I remember very little of the rest of the trip or of the ride back home. But that experience with the power of the Word of God I will never forget.

* * * *

Soon after writing the account of Wesley's Bethel experience and the victory over his tobacco habit, we went to a funeral.

The 52-year-old man (we'll call him Jeff) had died of cancer. When we viewed the body, I noticed someone had placed a packet of tobacco in his pocket along with a cap and some flowers.

A local pastor, David, had taken upon himself the burden of this man's soul. Because of David's concern and visits, Jeff, on his deathbed had received Christ in salvation.

David was in charge of the funeral. As a eulogy, he told this story.

"You all know Jeff liked his 'bakker' (chewing tobacco). Well, several days ago, when Jeff was real sick, he called his friend from his hospital bed. 'Friend,' he said, 'I need to ask a favor of you.'

'What is it? I'll do it.'

'I need some bakker.'

His friend made preparations to go to the hospital with some tobacco. But before he left the house, Jeff called again.

'You don't need to come.' His voice seemed stronger. 'I've got my bakker. A little boy come into my room, looked at me and asked me what I wanted. I told him I wanted some bakker. In just a little while, here he comes. He handed me a pack of bakker and left. I didn't see the boy no more; don't know who it was.'"

Pastor David concluded the eulogy, "I think God sent that little boy to ease a dying man's pain."

So there you have it. It seems ironical, yet our God is big enough to cleanse a young man from an addiction and to grant a dying man his request.

Screwdriver Angel

"No, you won't need your tool box on this trip," Wayne Sheffel had told me before we started out. "The truck has just been tuned. It'll run."

"But I always take my tool box, just in case." I wasn't convinced.

"Naw, you won't need it this time. Besides, there isn't room on the truck."

I should have listened to my intuition.

The 650-mile trip, in the middle of the night, was long and lonely and I was already tired. The day before, Wilford McGeary and I had loaded several hundred laboratory rabbits into a green ton stake-bed truck and drove to a rabbit market close to Philadelphia, Pennsylvania. We arrived in time to unload our cargo, grabbed a bite to eat and started back.

Traveling 1,300 miles, nonstop, can be formidable, but Wilford and I would "spell" each other sleeping and driving. Besides, we were driving a reliable borrowed vehicle—we thought.

Wilford was asleep and it was my turn to drive. It was 1:00 a.m. and we were on the Pennsylvania Turnpike, midway between Harrisburg and Breezewood, where we head south to Kentucky. Going up a long hill I pulled into the passing lane to pass several 18 wheelers. Halfway past them the old Ford truck lost power, misfiring on the hill and losing speed. I had to drop back and follow the trucks to the top of the hill. Down the other side I fretted, *Oh no! I don't have my tool box! I should have listened to my intuition. But now it's running fine; perhaps I won't need it.* On the next big hill I pulled out again to pass several trucks and one big rig pulled out behind me. Halfway up the hill it started losing power again, sagging slower and slower. I couldn't drop back because this big rig was right on my tail (or shall I say back bumper). I was embarrassed in this predicament because I've always tried never to kill a big rig's speed on a hill. "Stay out of their way!" is my motto. I tried to let the driver know I had trouble, but I couldn't. Finally I ducked between two rigs in the right lane and got on the shoulder. We ambled along at 30 miles per hour. *And I don't have a toolbox, not even a flashlight.* I drove on the shoulder for about 10 miles and started to pray. "Lord, help! Help me make it to a service bay before this rig quits, and please Lord, I need a mechanic on duty at 1:30 a.m. At the least I need a screwdriver and a flashlight, and perhaps a pliers." By this time my mind had deciphered that most likely the points in the distributor needed adjusting or replacing.

Up ahead was a service bay! Wilford was still asleep. The Ford was too crippled to run, so it limped into the service station. I got out and, oh joy, the door was open to the service bay, the lights were on and no other vehicle around! Hopefully we could get in. I saw all the tools hanging on the wall behind the work bench—screwdrivers and pliers and everything we would need in case there was no mechanic.

A young man was pumping gas. "Can I help you?"

I told him my story. "Is there a mechanic on duty?"

"No."

"Well, will you let me push this truck into the bay and use a few tools to fix it?"

"No. Had one in there last night that caught fire and the boss said absolutely no vehicles in there at night." *Please, Lord, I need a screwdriver and a light.* I turned to the service man.

"Could I borrow a few tools and a light from your bay?"

"No! The boss said absolutely no borrowing of tools—they don't come back. No tools to nobody." He looked at my worried face. Finally he said, "Look, this flashlight is mine, not the bosses'. If it's any help, take it and check out your truck." I said thanks to the man, and to the Lord I said, "What next? I sure need a screwdriver." To myself I said, "Where do I start? At the distributor." Wilford was still asleep. I loosened the friction springs on the distributor cap, picked it up and, with the light, found a place to put it on top of the engine block. **Right there**, where I placed the cap was a black-handled screwdriver! I looked at the thing, said, "Thanks, Lord," picked it up and got to work. Yes, the points were set too close; had heated up on a hard pull and shorted out. They weren't burned too badly, so with what Matthew Web calls my "micro-meter eye-ball," I set the points where they should be and replaced the cap. I slammed the hood, got into the cab (Wilford was still asleep), and turned the key. The old 302 engine roared to life and purred like a lion. Hallelujah! Thank you, Jesus! I took another look at the screwdriver in my hand. "Lord, tell the angel who brought that screwdriver, 'Thanks for the help.'"

I pulled around to the pumps to fill up with gas and said to the attendant, "Here's your flashlight and thanks so much."

"Fixed already?" he asked as he started gassing my truck.

"Tell 'im. Tell 'im." The Lord said.

So I told the attendant about the screwdriver. When I finished he was purely shaking. "Whew! That makes me shiver!"

I told him that makes me feel good all over because God knows all about me and cares for his children. "Are you one of his children?" He said he didn't have time to talk about it and left.

– CHAPTER 4 –

Bind Up the Brokenhearted

The Wake

What would I do without Jesus?
The Shepherd of my valley.
I couldn't make it without Jesus;
What would I do?

Bernie's strong voice and the strumming of his guitar blended with all the rest of the sounds of "The Wake." The noise of several dozen children playing, shouting, and running in and out of the church was getting louder even though it was nearly midnight. If they were tired, they didn't know it. Their little friend, eleven-year-old Darren, was dead and lying in his casket at the front of the church. He had been at school with them earlier that week. "I ate lunch with him," Jeff remembered. Now he was dead. Nobody knew for sure what happened, but his brother found him dead soon after he was home from school. He had choked, the coroner said.

These children, along with their parents and grandparents and dozens of cousins and friends, were participating in an age old funeral custom—The Wake. "We want to stay with Darren all night," his mother had said.

Fortunately it was a warm night in May. Our little church couldn't hold the crowd of people, so they wandered in and out of the building. Outside, they smoked and talked and hollered at the kids. Inside they ate and drank pop, visited and cried, examined the flowers, listened to the singers, and hollered at the kids. Always there was one or several at the casket, weeping and remembering. And hugging. Little Darren was nearly covered with flowers, cards, gifts his friends wanted to send with him, games, "I love you and will miss you" notes, pocket knives, and a can of Skoal tobacco. There was no doubt he was loved.

Downstairs in the fellowship room, the tables were full of a hodge-podge unorganized array of food. Organization is nearly impossible when people are eating non-stop all day and all night. There was bread and lunch meat, beans and potato salad, ham and fried chicken, potato chips galore, pies, cakes, moon pies and snack cakes, gallons of coffee, and dozens of cans of pop.

Earlier in the evening there had been a service. The Mennonites sang "Jesus Loves Me." G.C. McIntosh and his family had come all the way from Millers Branch, with their guitars and their babies, to sing some beautiful Heaven songs. Wesley sang "Supper Time." Anybody who would, sang a song or two to comfort the family. Wesley and Calvin and Brother McIntosh preached briefly. Wesley reminded us how tenderly Jesus cares for the children. "He took them up in his arms and blessed them. Don't send the children away. Bring them to Jesus."

Finally Prophet Boomer arrived. He preached a powerful gospel message and sang the Christian version of "Achy Breaky Heart." Then he gave an altar call. "There is no better time to come to Jesus," he said. Many of the people in this audience were unchurched and unsaved, and I experienced the same sad heavy burden that I often feel when an invitation is given to receive Christ's salvation and nobody responds.

Wesley often prays, "Lord, that this suffering and sorrow would not be in vain, that people would allow You to enter their broken hearts."

Darren's Aunt Sue Baker and her family were there. They were hurting. Only three weeks before, they were at this same church for the funeral of their husband and father. The grandparents were there too. Darren has two Papaws, a Mamaw, and a Great Mamaw. It hurts to lose a grandchild in death.

The front of the church was crowded with flowers and arrangements, teddy bears and angels. One of my favorite was a large framed-with-flowers picture of the Guardian Angel protecting two children on a broken bridge in a storm; also, a sculptured angel music box that played "Amazing Grace."

Toward morning, some went home for a few hours rest before the funeral service at 11:00 a.m. Mommy and Daddy stayed (Donald and Mary Johnson), along with Mamaw and some aunts and uncles and cousins. Some lay down on the carpet to sleep. Others kept the coffee brewing and cleaned up some of the food mess. Darren lay sleeping. The day of the funeral was extremely difficult for Donald and Mary and their other two sons. "I have dug many graves and I have helped to bury many people," Donald said. "But when it's your own, you just can't stand it."

Several days after the funeral, Donald and Mary came to see us with a letter of appreciation to post at the church. "I just couldn't believe all the people who helped in so many ways," Donald said. "We can't begin to thank everybody. Our family feuds and fights a lot, but when something like this happens, we all help each other."

"I didn't know if anybody would come to the funeral or if anyone would bring flowers," Mary added.

"That is what friendship and community is all about," Wesley told them. And I thought, *especially in this country, where people still care enough to stay up all night with their dead, who care enough to observe The Wake.*

Wesley prayed with them again and Donald said, "Give me a hug, Marthy." He is so tall I just grabbed his waist, looked in his face and said, "Now, because your heart is broken, is a good time to begin to seek the Lord."

"Mary and I were talking about that," he said.

Jesus Has a Rocking Chair

The message came while we were in Florida attending the funeral of Wesley's niece, Inez, in November 1999. "Ella May's week-old baby died. They don't know what happened, probably crib death. They want Wesley to have the funeral."

Immediately my mind skipped back a dozen years—the years when Elly Moore and Marsha Cole and I became good friends—a Sunday School teacher-pupil friendship. They let me ride their new bicycles and I tried to teach them to crochet. They called me Teddy Bear and I forget my pet names for them. Every Sunday morning for years we met in the basement classroom where I taught them of God's love and salvation, and about what's right and what's wrong. They loved me and I loved them. They engraved their names on the bulletin board, within a heart. At some point the names were scratched out and they quit Sunday School. The heart is still there.

I didn't see much of the girls after that. Because of some wrong choices, life hasn't been easy for them. But the heart is still there.

We couldn't be at the funeral, but after we got back home, I went to see Ella Mae. With pop cans in hand and cigarette smoke swirling over our heads (Marthy, you don't care if I smoke, do you?), I listened as Elly told me all about her beautiful and healthy baby, about the death of Amber and about the funeral. She showed me pictures and keepsakes. I knew she loved this baby, but she wasn't bitter, just sad. I assured her that Amber was safe with Jesus.

Two months later, Marsha's sister Diane, gave birth to a premature stillborn baby. Mr. Deaton placed Breanna Lee in a pretty little box and brought her to our church for a funeral. The night before, there was a service and all-night visitation. Some people call this a "wake." Once again many unbelievers heard the gospel message of salvation in Jesus Christ. Once again family and community were together to share in the grief of a young girl who must bury her baby. Wesley's grief was very deep. He was sharing in the sufferings of Jesus because so many people continue to reject Jesus Christ.

All night, people were in and out, eating, drinking coffee and Pepsi, and visiting. Children running and playing, crying with fatigue, and hyper with caffeine. Many left after 1:00 a.m. but several stayed on. Some slept a little, stretched out on a pew or on the floor in the nursery. Diane's boyfriend's mother was so weary. Toward morning Wesley found a pillow for her. "Here's a pillow for you. Why don't you sleep some on this back bench?"

Ella Mae was there. She and Diane cried when we sang, "Safe in the Arms of Jesus." At one point a visitor walked in carrying a baby. Ella jumped up. "Oh! Look at that pretty baby. Do you think they will let me hold it?" They did and she smiled through her tears.

After midnight, Wesley brought me home and he returned to the church for several more hours. I went into our bedroom, collapsed onto the bed and cried. I wept for the young girls who must bury their babies. I wept for the dozens of "our" girls who are hurting because of their wrong choices. I thought of the pain that comes when abortion happens, whether natural or induced, and I thought of the many tears shed at those times and for years after. I remembered how devastated our daughter and daughter-in-law were after a miscarriage.

"Oh God," I prayed, "have mercy on those many women. Somehow, may they know there is healing and hope because of Jesus. Amen."

*God's love is unconditional. No matter who you are or what you have done or will do, no matter where you go or don't go, no matter if you pray or don't pray, no matter if you worship Him or not, you can **never** escape God's love. However, God's love alone will not get you to Heaven. Forgiveness will. But forgiveness is* *conditional. You are forgiven by God **if** you acknowledge your sinfulness and humbly ask forgiveness.*

Good Old Country Boy

> *Go rest high on that mountain,*
> *Son, your work on earth is done.*
> *Go to Heaven a shouting,*
> *Look for the Father and the Son.*

"He was just a good old country boy." We were buying flowers at Town and Country Florist and were on our way to J.D. Turner's funeral. The florist was arranging flowers and remembering J.D. "Just a good old country boy," she repeated.

His life exemplified a twentieth century mountain man. "Hard work never killed nobody," he would say. "Dreading it will." J.D. lived in the era when his father's mules were replaced by a tractor. A preacher at his funeral recalled the miles and miles and miles J.D. rode his tractor, farming the river bottoms, leaving home early and coming back late. He often had cattle and big gardens. Instead of government hand-outs, he worked hard to make life a little easier for Louette and the children. No, hard work didn't kill J.D—cancer did.

He took a strong, almost arrogant stand on some doctrines of the Bible. It got him into disagreements with other church people at times, but no matter—"You can say what you want and argue all day, but this is what I believe, because this is what the BIBLE says, regardless of your 'nomination.'" He was ordained to preach by a Full Gospel preacher and was a member of the Church of God. He preached and sang at various churches and memorial meetings. He never doubted his salvation because it was based on the shed blood of Jesus Christ. A good old country boy who believed the Bible literally.

"You're livin' above your raisin'," is an accusation we sometimes hear against a person who gets a big education and lives fancy and gets the "big head." That could never be said of J.D. He was a natural for the country. He lived on a very small farm and didn't know about vacations. I doubt he had a hankering to travel much outside of Breathitt County. Bib overalls suited him very well. Which is not to say he was perfect. In his younger years alcohol was a problem. His father was a man of rage and perhaps J.D. learned some of that. However, humility means we don't deny our past sins; neither do we glory in them or glamorize them. We place them under the blood of Jesus. So before a huge crowd of friends and acquaintances of J.D. and his family, preacher Gary Bellamy could say with confidence, "You don't have to worry about this man. He was ready to go."

As Wesley and I followed the family to the top of the mountain, the words of this song followed—the song that was sung three times at the funeral.

Go rest high on that mountain,
Son, your work on earth is done.

It takes a high tenor voice for that song. Mose Turner has it.

In September there will again be a memorial meeting on the top of that mountain. Possibly that song will be sung. J.D., the Good Old Country Boy, is resting high on that mountain. His work is done.

Four months later, November 29, 2000, J.D.'s son, Robert J., died suddenly at the age of 52. He was buried beside his father. His mother was heartbroken and there is one more grief-stricken widow.

– CHAPTER 5 –

The Way It Was

Some call it the "Good Old Days" and recall with fondness the "Simple Life." Others remember the hardships and deprivations. Regardless of how it is described, life in Breathitt County and surrounding places sixty years ago was extremely interesting and worth recording.

Across the Hills and Down the Hollers
by Will Johnson

I interviewed Will in September, in the middle of the ginseng season. He had just come in from "sangin'." "Will, you are an old hand at digging ginseng. Tell me, how do you find it?"

When you're huntin' for ginseng, there's a certain kind of weed—I don't know what you call it—when you see that weed, you'll find sang, but if you don't see any of them weeds, you need'nt look for it. I ginsenged all my life. Sure have, one hillside to another. See, right now, it's not too dangerous for snakes. But when it's real hot, you don't go out in the hills by yourself. I almost stepped on rattlesnakes two or three times. I sure have. I was down here on George's Branch in a holler, me and Frank White. We went up this holler. I was in front of Frank and there was a big old root, U shaped, and it was full of leaves. I laid my hand up on a rock and raised my foot to step down on the root. When I started to set my foot down, I looked and there was a big rattlesnake, coiled up, with its head stickin' up, just like that! If I'd put my foot down, hit'ud got me right there.

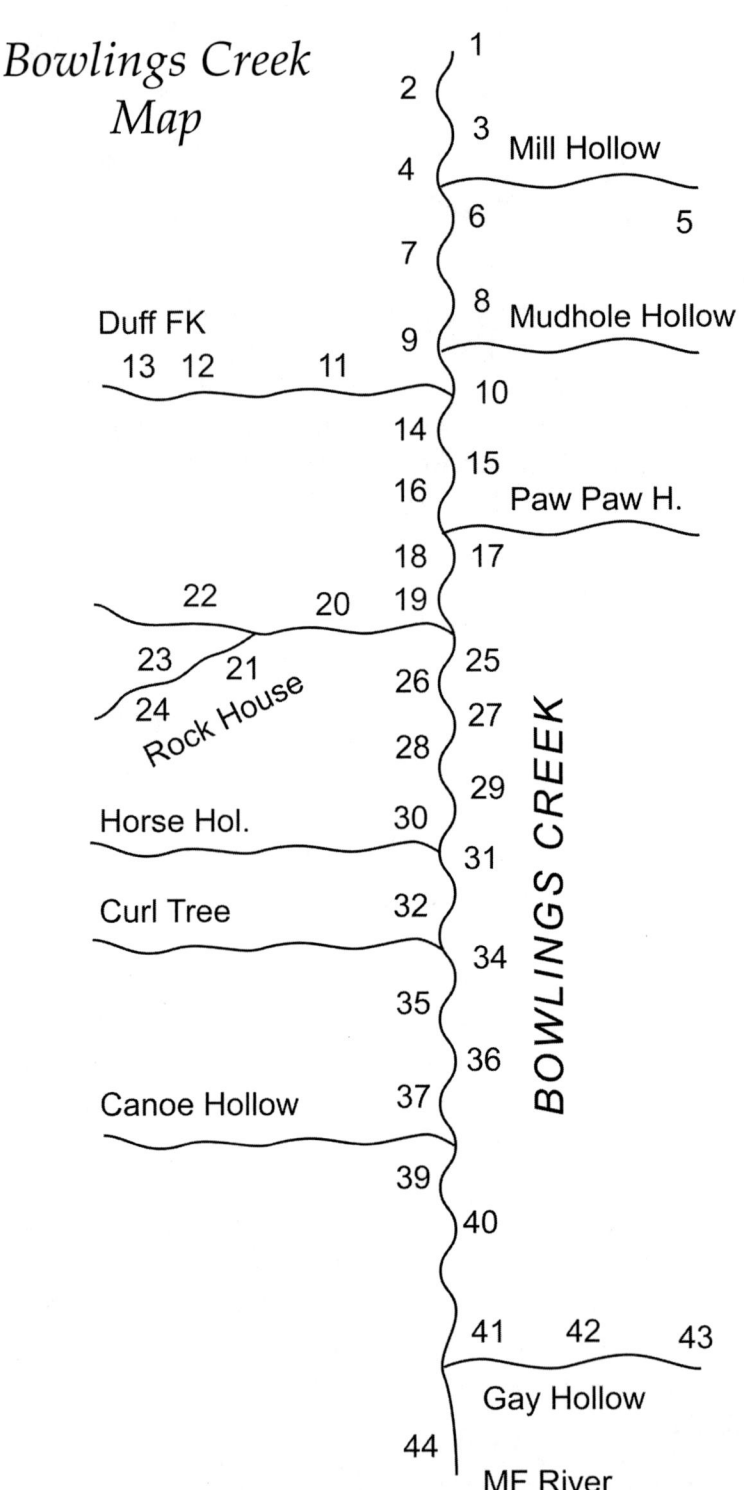

Families living along the Bowlings Creek in the 1920s and 1930s as remembered by Woodrow W. Deaton:

1. Alex Turner
2. Billy Turner
3. Johny Turner
4. Rodge Herald
5. Sam Turner and Johny Bowling
6. Jesse Turner
7. Sam Turner
8. Greenbertty Turner
9. James C. Deaton
10. Charley Turner
11. John A. Deaton
12. James "Cub" Herald
13. James G. Deaton
14. Jesse Spicer
15. Abe Spicer
16. Sallie Spicer
17. Jess Spicer
18. John D. Adams and Shade Spicer
19. Ed. Deaton and Gran Riley (P.O. site ca1935)
20. Harlan Burton and Ossle Turner (P.O. site from 1937-1945)
21. Brant Deaton
22. Lewis Noble and Ed. E. Deaton
23. Ossie E. Turner
24. John J. Bowling
25. Joe C. Raleigh
26. Charlie Burton and Shade Spicer
27. Bobby Johnson
28. Elisha Baker and Pearl Combs
29. School District #56
30. Ancil Cole
31. Ula B. Johnson
32. George Johnson and Robert Johnson (site of first Beech P.O. ca1927/28
33. Clint Chandler
34. Lewis Baker and John J. Bowling
35. Hacker Combs
36. Bryan Turner
37. Lewis Deaton and Russel Asher
38. Willie Pruitt
39. Craig Combs and Floyd Noble
40. Levi Combs
41. Harlan Johnson
42. John L. Combs
43. Nathan "Curly" Combs
44. Rob Combs

Rob Combs and Elly, you knew them, didn't you? They ran a grocery store—now that was back in the 1930's. Don't know what year, but it was in the Hoover days. Rob would get groceries from Pal Hackman in Jackson. The groceries would come out to Altro on the Local (train). He'd travel the seven miles to meet the Local and pick up his groceries, with his mule and wagon. Well, anyhow, one day it was real, real cold. We lived down there where you all have church. Rob came up the road with his wagon. Now when it was real cold, Rob walked behind the wagon—mules knowed the way just as good as he did. He came up the road and stopped there at our house. I was just a little boy. He stopped and he told my Daddy, he said, "I got dog bit down the road a while ago."

"Where 'bouts?"

"Down there by the Horse Holler." Said that dog just trotted up behind him and reached out and grabbed him by the hand. He told my Daddy, "If that dog comes up here, kill it and cut its head off." At that time dogs were awful bad about going mad. They'd go mad—just crazy. But anyhow, Rob went on and a little while later, that dog come trottin' up the road and went right up in under the floor (of our house). We had a big lot of chickens under there and that dog went up under there and was bitin' them chickens and them just a squawkin'! That dog got wedged behind the chimney. We put on a kettle of water, got it boiling and killed that dog. My Daddy took that dog out to the creek and laid it on ice. It was so cold and the ice on the creek so thick that it could hold a pair of miles. He chopped the dog's head off and when Rob come back with his wagon, he give it to him, in an 8-pound bucket. He took it to Jackson to have it tested and it was mad (rabid). Rob had to go and take so many shots, and he got alright.

You were young when your Mother died, weren't you?

I was four years old when my Mother died. The only thing I can remember when Mother died was this: Alice Turner, now I don't know if you ever knew her or not, she married Charlie Turner, and they lived down there where Bill Willett lives. (*Will got choked up at this point.*) A whole lot of this stuff I just absolutely forgot. But Alice Turner, she lifted us children up. The casket was settin' in the house. She lifted us children up to look at our Mother. Sister Effie was about two and a half years old. My mother died of what they called heart dropsy. She was 32. From that time—it was a right smart while—it was just us children, you know. We never had a stepmother then. Much later, my Daddy married Marthy.

Times was hard. We could feed the chickens through the kitchen floor. My Daddy worked on WPA (a government program). It paid about 8 dollars every two weeks. He was working over at Altro on the road. We had a horse. We boys would take him to work and bring the horse back for us to use all day, then go back and pick him up.

We had chickens and mules and hogs, and we raised corn in that holler across from where you have your church. I'll tell you a good un'. We had a horse—a Percheron, a big horse, a good one. We'd take our Daddy to work on the WPA and we'd bring that horse back to plow. We'd plow awhile and fight awhile. Me and Wilson would. (Wilson was my twin brother.) We would . . . we'd plow awhile and fight awhile! We knowed if we didn't plow, our Daddy would whip us. We'd fight sometimes 2 or 3 times a day and then get back to work (*time out here for a chuckle*).

Times was hard. We just had to do the best we could. Our neighbor was a schoolteacher, but he had no feelings for us five motherless children. He had his land posted "No trespassing." But us boys went over there squirrel huntin'. The neighbor found out and got a warrant out for us boys. When the sheriff came, it was Robert Amis. Did you know him? He saw us boys were just children and he wouldn't serve the warrant. But my brothers got even with the neighbor. He had a big bunch of sheep, and let them run free, everywhere they wanted. My brother caught one of his sheep and put it in our barn and went and got the sheriff. Our neighbor had to pay two dollars and a half to get his sheep back. That was more than the sheep was actually worth! (*Sweet revenge!*)

In 1939 there came a big rain—a wash-out. I went over to Altro to bring my Daddy home from work on the WPA. We came up the hollow, we called it George Mullins Hollow then. People came across that hill right there and across the hollow, and down through Duff Fork. That was a shortcut from going all the way around, you see. We started up that holler and it come a fast cloud over, a real fast one, and all at once it began to pour the rain. I mean, it just came a wash-out, you know. We tied that horse up, in the holler and we jumped off and went in a barn, out of the storm. It was a slick, rocky holler and after a long time of hard rain, we heard rocks tumbling down that holler, real loud. We walked out there to the edge of the bank and that holler had washed out all around our horse and his legs was just a goin' up and down! Well, it got dark on us 'cause we had to wait till the creeks went down. We got the horse and went on up to Andy Cranks. We went in that house and, boy, I was froze to death! I was just a little feller and I was cold and wet. That old woman, she built a fire in there and she went and got supper, and I thought I never will forget that. I never have. Rosie Crank, that's who it was. It was way in the night and we came on across that hill, and I'm tellin' you what, the holler was washed out so bad you could hardly get in and out. We finally got on home. When we got there, we saw our barn had washed away!

I don't believe we had a clock part of the time. But we had chickens, to crow. On a certain time every morning they started to crow. When it crowed the second time, that was 2:00. That's when my Daddy got up and got something to eat and went on to work. They'd leave at 4:00 every morning and go on to Canoe.

My Grandpa lived at Altro, down across the railroad, down there. Everybody had a big bunch of children and we'd go to their house. We'd just go back and forth to everybody's house. John and Jane Baker was my Mother's parents. Some of them worked in the coal mines. My Daddy worked in the coal mines too, over at Barwick, a long, long time. The coal tipple burned up and they had to quit. Anyhow, we'd go to our Grandpa's over there. They had two big old rooms and we children would play blindfold. Oh, we had one of the awfullest good times ever was. That old woman (Grandma) would be sittin' there before the fire, her hair draggin' the floor, might near. Our playing didn't bother her one speck. And she'd get up in the morning and she baked them biscuits that big a-round! That was just as good as eating fried chicken. Yeah, they were real good to us. Three of their daughters died at the age of 32.

How was Christmas special?

Well, most everybody was lucky to get anything. But anyhow, at Christmas, we usually got a cap buster. . . . I believe they cost a dime. A few caps in them. We got one of them and we'd get so much candy, you know. And our Daddy would hole up apples till Christmas too, when we were children. We'd always had a good Christmas dinner. Not like they do now, but it was good. Isobel (my older sister) did the cooking. She started cooking when she was just a little girl, when our Mother died.

What about school days?

I really didn't go to school every day, but the school was right there below us. We went about half time and I went to the eighth grade, just enough to get by. I'll tell you what we would do. On Friday evening they'd always give out candy. We'd make a special effort to be there Friday evening. Well, I went to school to Sam P. Deaton. He was a good teacher. And Kelly Herald, you ever heard tell of him? He was a good teacher too. And I went to school to Greenbury Turner's girl, the one married Sam Herald. Kathryn was her name.

The first car I ever saw in my life . . . we lived right there where you all lived at. Bob Deaton and some of his boys came up through the road there with an A Model Ford. It went put-put-put-put-put. And it was the awfullest looking thing I ever saw in my life.

It was! That was a funny looking thing. I don't know how they got it across that hill. There were no roads across the Wolf Creek Hill, over there. But it came up that road, just a chuggin' along. Yes, sir!

Only way we traveled when I was a boy was by horse or mule, one. There were more roads (trails) across these hills and around these ridges then there were right down here on the level. You could start up the hill down here where Roscoe's girl lives, or up Duff Fork, and come out on Turners Creek. You go down Lick Branch or Wolf Creek—that was a shortcut. I don't think I went to Jackson or Hazard till I was about 15 years old. You had to go by train. It was five mile from where we lived to the train station at Altro. We rode a horse over there and Owen Moore had a barn close to the station. He charged a quarter a day to leave your horse.

What did they do when anyone got sick?

We had home remedies. I'll tell you what they did for measles. They'd go to the cliff where a sheep had been and get the manure. They'd boil it and give it to the children to break the measles out. Another thing, like if somebody had a goiter on their neck . . . I believe there was an old man down the river across from Cam's Branch over there. He could take them off. My sister Effie had one and it sure did leave her. I don't know what he did. Another thing they did, like if a baby had the thrash *(sore mouth)*, the seventh boy in a family would blow in its mouth. You ever heard of that? They could cure it.

Yeah, there were some mean people and some good 'uns. I'll not tell no names, but anyhow, my Dad was up in the Rock House Holler plowing, getting ready to plant corn, you know. Well, I had gone somewhere else. Some man came up there and told my Dad, "I'm gonna kill Will." And I had done nothin' to him noway! So, when he left, my Dad came and got me. When we came out of that holler and came down the road, we ran into him—him and another man by the name of Johnny. He was a good old feller. They were both drinking. They got into a fight, right there in the road. That feller told us, "I'm goin' home and get my gun and I'm gonna kill every one of you." We never said a word to him and just came on to the house. He went on home. So help me, God, if he didn't come back. Now I had a gun and Wilson had one and Dad had one. We saw him come up the road. It was just a dirt road then, you know. He had a .22 gun. He came in front of our house and shot right over top of the door. When he did that, I stepped out in the yard and he shot right over top of my head. Well, Daddy shot at him, Wilson did and I did too. He fell down like he was dead. All at once he jumped up and run up that road a flyin'. He went on up the road where Malvery Deaton lived. She had a pair of mules. She rode mules just like a man. He told Malvery, "I'm going back down the road to my house. If they kill me goin' back down there," he said, "you bring the wagon and take me home." Anyhow, we saw him come back down the road. We had our guns on him, every step he made. He came right down the road and never raised his head up. Well, if he had, we would have killed him, 'cause we was afraid not to. Now, when he wasn't drinking, he was as good a feller you ever saw. But he was dangerous, he sure was.

    When we were growing up, we worked for Ned Deaton and Sim Jett and Robert Johnson. You knowed Robert Johnson, didn't you? Plowing or hoeing corn or laying by corn or whatever. We boys got 50 cents a day and our Dad got 75 cents a day. Hargas Cole, Jerry Cole, Stella, me and Wilson, all worked for Sim Jett. Ned paid us in meat. And Kathryn Turner was good to us too. When we worked all day, gee, it was hot! . . . we stopped by Kathryn's house and she gave us a gallon of milk to take home. That helped. We didn't have a Mother, you know, and times was hard. But after World War II, things went to pickin' up. Money began to raise up to a dollar and a half a day and then three dollars, you know. Things started blooming.

    All three of us boys passed for the army. I spent two years in France and Germany and came on home. Then I married Mima Noble and moved to Franklin, Ohio, and then to Dayton. I worked out there 18 years. Mima died when our children were small.

We did a lot of walkin'. I worked on the MYA one time (a government job, cutting timber), at Quicksand and Lost Creek. At the end of a day's work we'd get a ride to Haddix and catch the evening train to Altro and walk on home. One Friday evening, we missed the train. It had been gone only five minutes. There we were, stuck to walk, from Haddix to Bowlings Creek (15 or 20 miles up hills and down hollows). Well, anyhow, we started walking, it was the only choice we had. It got dark on us and we got over here to the mouth of Wolf Creek. Joe Raleigh's old woman fixed us a bottle light. You don't know what a bottle light is? You take something like a pint bottle and fill it full of coal oil and put a rag down in there, and let it stick up so much and let it burn. We came on home by the light of that bottle light. I'll tell you what's the truth, I never was so tired in my whole entire life. I didn't think I'd ever make it, but we did. That was a long walk after workin' hard all day.

What about church life?

Well, at that time, the biggest single group through here was the Baptists. I don't know what kind it was, there's different names for Baptists. But anyhow, they used the school house down on Bowlings Creek for a church house. This old feller, this real old feller, he'd sit back in the church house and he had a walkin' stick. And he, when the children got too rough, he'd grab ahold of that cane and Buddy, he'd set 'em down! But anyhow, I remember one time when I was just a child, they were taking turns preaching. And this one feller got up to preach and this other old feller sitting up in a front seat, he told him, he said, "I want you to sit down! Let Charlie preach awhile." That was Charlie Turner.

I'll tell you another thing. Tommy Baker had gone to Hazard and he "made" a Holiness preacher. And some of those Holiness people came down to the school-church. And when they

Ervin Graber and Beulah Spicer at Gays Creek.

came, they brought along a colored woman. She was big, real big. That was the first colored person I ever saw in my life. And she'd go through that church house a singing and praising the Lord. Us children would get behind the door and watch her.

We'd go to graveyard meetings too. They'd ride mules over to Gays Creek, or go to the head of Lick Branch over here and go up that holler where my Dad lived at, and go to the top of that hill on the Lick Branch side, and you'd go over there to church. There would be a BIG crowd of people . . . horses and mules tied all around the cemetery. They sure would. A dozen or more preachers, and they'd take time about preachin'. That cemetery used to be the prettiest place you ever saw in your life, at the head of Lick Branch. It was at the head of nowhere but it was pretty. It sure was. If you go through there now, you don't know there's a cemetery there. It's growed up in briars and the fence rotted down.

Let me tell you what . . . I want you to put in your book that I like to hunt for ginseng!

Will Johnson lives with his wife, Linda, in a trailer home at the head of Bushes Branch, with many of his children close by. Will and Linda and their extended family have been, and still are our very good friends. Their roots reach deep into the Breathitt County Hills.

Mommy the Matriarch
by Mose Turner

My Mother gave birth to all nine of us kids at home. The rest of us were never allowed to be at the house when that happened. The babies were all "caught" at home by a midwife.

Caught?

Yeah, that's what mountain people called it. Mommy and Daddy kept the facts of life from us little children. Of course the facts were distorted. I asked Daddy why the baby can't walk, and why does that woman carry that big black bag? "Well, she's got a little black dog in that bag. It runs that baby down to catch it and then it breaks its legs so it can't walk."

Mommy always had feather beds. Man, they were warm, but they were hard to make with goose down. Every so often we would pluck the geese. Mom would catch the goose and put the head under her arm. Then she'd get the two feet and tuck them under the tail feathers to expose the chest. Then she'd start ripping. Every time she'd pluck, the old goose would say, "Bwack!" Pluck. "Bwack!" Pluck. "Bwack!" In a few months they would feather back out, then they were ready for pluckin' again. That's an old saying, "Ready to be plucked again."

The women always had white muslin cloth on hand. When someone died, the neighbor women started immediately sewing a gown and would take the muslin cloth to line the coffin. There was a saw mill in every community. So when they sawed a real big yeller Poplar log, they would always lay up those wide boards in a barn loft to be seasoned out, so when somebody died, they used that lumber. There was always someone who could make a coffin. One board made the bottom and one on each side and they would shape it at the shoulders and narrow it at the feet. They buried them just as soon as they could, 'cause I've seen where you had to keep the flies minded away from them. No mortician, just a neighborhood effort.

We had very few amusements when I was growing up. Some of us had an old battery operated radio. We couldn't get much of nothing on it and sometimes the battery would get weak and they would put it in the oven and heat it up. But I do remember that everybody was faithful to the Grand Ole Opry. And I can remember so plain, listening to Joe Lewis the boxer. My Mommy would listen to the war news and it told of so many hundred getting killed, and oh how that would grieve her. I used to listen to Amos and Andy, the colored comedians. One of the Westerns I listened to was the Lone Ranger—all those sound effects was something!

My Daddy never did, but lots of men were involved in making moonshine with homemade stills. People were poor and desperate for some extra money. Some of the women said the moonshine money never went nowhere nohow. But Ancil Cole didn't have to make moonshine, he had a government job. I remember that Ancil carried the mail from Altro to the Beech post office, about five miles, over the hills and through the creeks, on his mule. And that snow, you know, where he'd go through the creek and splatter that water on him, I'd see ice froze to his knees. He wore them big army overcoats, they were that green real fuzzy heavy stuff. Finally he got a truck and just started driving it. He didn't know a thing about driving it. He'd put the gas to the floor and set and hold that clutch and he finally let it out. Why, he'd run it in low gear all the way to Altro. I don't see why in the world he never got killed.

That stone rock school building at Altro. . . . In WPA days they cut those stone, big as this room, out of rock from up in that holler. They cut them without power equipment of any kind, just hammers and chisels and wedges. That was my alma mater and I came back to teach there in 1963. But first I attended Bowlings Creek one-room school. Back then 16 or 17 year olds would be in grade school. They just went to school sorta when they wanted to, or when they couldn't work on the farm. Some teachers couldn't handle them. When they'd try to discipline them, the student would grab the paddle and sling the teacher around. They just weren't tough enough to handle those big overgrown boys. There were other teachers, though, tough enough to handle them. They'd beat the boys real hard. See, you never heard of child abuse. For some, that was the only language they could understand. One teacher was so mean, I was scared of him. I remember when I went to bed wishing I could die that night so I wouldn't have to go to school.

When it came dinner time at school . . . there were always several from one family attended the one-room school, and each family brought lunch for all, in one bucket. We just brought what we raised and ate at home: biscuit and egg sandwiches, corn bread, roastin' ears, green beans (cold, of course). Sometimes meat between a biscuit. Sometimes we brought just a whole bucket of crumbled up milk and bread (corn bread). And we would go out around the school to eat. There was a big flat rock and a lot of Beech trees with roots you could sit on. And I remember you couldn't hardly eat for Ancil Cole's half starved dogs and chickens. They'd run right up and try to grab it right out of your hands! This one family they'd about fight every time they'd eat, you know, one would try to get it all.

We played an hour after dinner. We'd play base and tag and foxes and dogs. We'd play stick ball. No competitive teams. No organized sports whatsoever and no sports equipment. And we never said we're bored and got nothing to do.

How did we get to school? We walked two and one-half miles, all of us together. Most of the time when the weather was warm we walked barefooted, but, now, we always did have shoes for winter. Daddy would sell a calf or save fodder for the neighbors (for a little pay) for shoes. Walking to school, most of the road was through the creek but there was always a little walking path where you scaled around the bank, but you had to cross the creek occasionally and I remember sometimes I'd get my foot wet and, you know, those little gum boots, you'd get water in them and they'd go "squash squash" all day long and when you came home that night your foot would be just real wrinkly! If it was cold water, well, that was just tough.

One winter I had whooping cough, measles, mumps, bronchitis, and asthma all in one winter. Mommy failed me that year. The teacher didn't, but Mommy said, "You missed too much to learn what you were supposed to learn. You tell that teacher I said to keep you back."

One teacher was a young single lady. A young man from up the creek would sometimes come to the school to take her home on his mule. She'd get up sidesaddle and ride behind him. Well, his little cousin got mad, cause now he had to walk and the teacher got to ride, and he rocked them (threw rocks).

If you went to high school, you had to walk or ride in the back of a truck, down Bushes Branch to Altro, and catch the train to Jackson. It was a good ride. The seats were plushy, like a couch, and you could turn them around to face each other to play cards or whatever. It was an experience—about 45 minutes or an hour. The train stopped at Wolf Coal, Whick, Copeland. "All off for Altro!"

Now, Mose, what motivated you to get a high school and college education?

Well, Mommy always said, "Make something of yourself! You see how it is here, digging in these rocks. You can't make a living here." Besides, Eva Jean's Daddy was sending her to college.

I didn't want to just dig in the dirt while she was a teacher! Another thing motivated me; I went up to Northern Kentucky several summers. I had this cheap job right in the middle of Cincinnati, just like a slum . . . and that smell, I mean, you know, working like a dog and that smell! And living in a third floor apartment and it hot as fire. See, stuff like that—that made me want to go back to school.

First thing we did when we came from school was change clothes. We had one pair of good clothes and the rest were patched. My Mommy would take a switch and whip us if we abused our good clothes. One day Uncle Johnny . . . they had a team of mules and a wagon and they would cut their own logs. It was the time of year when the sap was in the trees, you see. They had cut a bunch of poplars and they'd skin the bark off those poplar logs to make them pull easier. The bark came off just like half the log, like a big trough. So one Sunday we boys had some sliding fun. We'd pour water down the mountain path and lay a piece of bark upside down and get on that bark slide. Then we would slide down the mountain, a long ways right down the mountain! I got my good clothes wet and dirty and my mother said, "Son, looks like you've been a loggin'." She whipped me too.

The first "brought-on" coat I could ever remember having, Sister Gertrude Dutcher brought it up to me. When they first settled this creek, you know, they parked their car over at Brown Combs. That was as far as a car could come. They'd always have a good horse. They had one named Bird and they had a Buckskin, you know, like a chocolate, black mane and tail. They rode fast too, 'cause they came out of Michigan where they were used to riding cars, and then when they got on their horses, it was "the farther the faster" up and down that creek, a bailin' them mud holes dry! But anyhow, she brought me my first little "brought-on" coat and that tickled me to death. She had some clothes in a sack, laying across the saddle and that little coat was sort of a herringbone-like, fuzzy-like, a dark maroon, sorta different shades of maroon, zipped up, short, with a band around the waist.

Soon as we changed into old clothes, we had to do chores. Some of us carried in wood, some coal or water or kindlin'. We always milked several cows. Sometimes we had to save fodder or we would go to the field and pick large meal sacks full of green beans. There'd be the awfullest pile of beans on the floor at the house and we'd all work them up at night. But you couldn't do enough work to suit my mother and that set of people; they were hard workers. But, you raise nine children on a rocky hillside and no income; if you were "sorry" (lazy) you starved. One family, it was said, ate kraut three times a day. But we worked hard and always had plenty of food. Our table was 8 or 10 feet long and it was always plumb full of food.

My Daddy had a tender heart, but Mommy believed in the biblical advice, "Spare the rod and spoil the child." Once when she was whipping me, Daddy said, "Woman, don't kill that child just for smokin'." She turned on him and said, "Don't you interfere when I'm disciplining my children!" Then she laid a couple on him! Daddy's brothers never let him forget that.

Mommy was an excellent reader and speller. The way she got her education was this: her daddy died when she was real young. Her uncle, to keep her from marrying Daddy, sent her to Berea to grade school. They still wound up getting married and she got educated too.

She was a hard worker. She went in the field with us and worked till 11:00 and came out to get dinner. We'd eat and lay around while she did the dishes. Then we'd all go back. She was like a slave driver. She pushed Daddy, and was a lot more energetic than he was. She'd tell us kids, "Son, if you hoe only 10 hills of corn, do it good." She was the one decided which field to hoe, and we quit pickin' berries only when we'd reach into the briers and fall over the cliff! I never could pick huckleberries—they were so good, if you put one in your mouth, you couldn't put anymore in your bucket.

We didn't have a refrigerator so we had to set our milk and butter down in the spring. Groundhog meat and squirrel meat was special. Mommy used a rub board to wash our clothes for years and years. Life was a struggle for Mother, with two or three little ones all the time. I've heard them say, to take care of a toddler, they took its little dress and lifted the bed stead up and set it down on the dress tail so they couldn't crawl out of the house. If we had taken better care of Mommy, she might have lasted longer.

The only church life was at the cemeteries. Like, you had a yearly meetin', sometimes it would start on Friday and go through Sunday. Then they gathered at different people's houses to eat. At other times preachers would come to somebody's house to have church. Willie Turner, he'd come to our house. Especially when old people would get down sick, like Uncle Billy, they'd always go and have meetin' for them. But there was no organized church when I was real young. When I got bigger and started walking with the girls, some of the Holiness Churches had buildings. Sometimes we walked plumb down Feb Fork and up Gays Creek to a Holiness Church.

We didn't go to church much but our parents taught us morals. If we did anything out of the way, Mommy would switch us no end. She never allowed fighting or foul language. She wore me to a frazzle for smoking. Mommy would read the Bible. (We always had a Bible.) Daddy was very religious but he couldn't read. But he knew most of the Bible by heart, just by hearing preachers preach it. My Dad never got drunk or cussed. He did smoke and chew tobacco, and Mommy hated that with a passion. Later he helped organize the Church of Christ on Bowlings Creek and was a faithful member the rest of his life.

You know, they got along real well, the different denominations. Before we had churches, they would have meetings in the one-room schoolhouse. They might preach a revival for a week, two or three different denominations at the same place. They might have 10 or 25 converts that week and on Sunday they'd all go down to the river. Some would want Eva Jean's Father, Henley Turner (a Baptist preacher), to baptize them, and some wanted Jesse Hall (a Church of Christ preacher), to baptize them. That way they got along good.

But seem like in the latter years people got set in their ways and think their church is the best.

What about your courtship with Eva Jean, Mose?

Well, I'll tell you, I started driving real early, about 15, 'cause my oldest brother John, when he went to Newport to work, he bought us a '55 Chevrolet pickup. I'd drive all of us to church at the old schoolhouse on Turners Creek. Well, we went to this one Memorial Meetin'. When I first met Eva Jean and first sorta looked at her and she kinda caught my eye, she was carrying her little baby brother on her hip, you know how they straddled the hip like that? She was pretty young then, about 12 or 13. But we didn't get married 'til I was a senior in college and she was a junior in high school. She was a cheerleader in a green jumper with a lot of pleats in it. When they'd spin, that would go around and around.

Eva Jean's Daddy talked about changing jobs on the highway and moving to another county. My Daddy said to me, "Boy, if you want that girl, you better get her 'fore she moves off." So I did. Eva Jean justified her marrying so young by saying, "When I was in grade school my Mommy was very sick, so Daddy and I had to do all the housework. That way I grew up fast."

Life was so rough in these mountains; no way to get any money. Just as soon as anyone got old enough, they'd find a way to get to Newport or Cincinnati to work. Life was rough, but you always wanted to come back. My brother Frank lived and worked in Ohio for 30-40 years and every time he would come home he said it's like going to a funeral when he had to leave again. Some leave and never come back. But that's just the way it is—a few people leave this country and never get it out of their system. And others leave it and don't ever want to come back.

Mose Turner, with his parents Bill and Lizzie, and his 8 siblings, grew up at the head of Bowlings Creek. He and his wife, Eva Jean, both taught for many years in Breathitt County schools.

They are retired and still live on Bowlings Creek, very close to where Mose grew up. They are active in the Bowlings Creek Church of Christ and have a singing ministry. Their two children and four grandchildren live close by.

I'm Proud of My Heritage
by Willie Johnson

We had a big garden and, like I said, I was at an age when I wasn't big enough to join the adults in all their work, you know. So my job was to feed all the animals and to get up all the wash water Mom needed. She did all the laundry on a washboard, you know, and she had a battin' stick. Have you heard of a battin' stick? Well, a battin' stick was a piece of wood that was kinda whittled down, to where it was kinda like a paddle. When the clothes was real dirty, she would put them in the water, maybe boil them a little, lay them on a rock and hit them with that battin' stick.

The Lord gave us so many different ways of surviving. Our forefathers . . . we look at them sometimes and say they weren't too educated or too bright, but they were! They learned how to do everything to survive. And they were very intelligent. We could dry food or can it or put it in a hole in the ground, you know, all different ways. My job was to put all the beans on the roof to dry, and all the apples we had peeled. You can dry that stuff and it won't spoil no way.

Sometimes on television and from society, you hear Kentucky and Tennessee kinda put down, if you know what I mean. They do; they talk about us pretty bad. I don't like it; I'm proud of my heritage.

Sometimes some of our young people have gone wild—on this dope and everything else. They claim it's peer pressure. They have to go to these places to get help to get off that stuff. I tell them, "Son, if you would spend time in the church like you're spending here, or some of the time on your knees," I said, "you wouldn't have to come here," you know. It's just a sign of the times. We can't give up hope on them. I just keep a prayin'.

How do you make sweet potato hills?

Well, some people make ridges now. We always made hills, not ridges. You had to rake the dirt all around it, to make a hill (*about two feet high and two feet across*), then flatten the top off to where you could plant a sweet 'tater slip that you had raised in a bed. We used to make lots of sweet 'tater hills. Gee, I guess we made a hundred, according to how big a patch we could crowd it into. Everything had to be crowded all you could. We didn't have too much flat ground, you know. The corn . . . you had to dig it in with a hoe, you know. Sometimes you had to reach down hill to get a hoe full of dirt to take up there to cover the seed.

I'm really proud of my heritage. Even though we were poor, we had a lot of love in the family. We usually had meals and you had to labor pretty hard. We never starved but we never had a real lot of stuff to eat either. There were eight of us boys around the table and one girl and Mom and Dad. The youngest was born after we all moved to Ohio.

If some of the older boys were out working or gone to the post office or something, when the rest of us ate supper, Mom would put their portion up in the warmin' closet of the old fashioned cook stove. And no matter how hungry one of us kids were or how much we would have liked to have that food, nobody would ever touch it—it would be there for whoever it belonged to. Like I said, we were poor.

But we had a lot of good neighbors; everybody was in the same boat. I remember we used to go to the fields to pick beans. We had what we called "meal" sacks, which were about as long as a "coffee" sack and half that long again. We'd pick those bags, three or four of them full of beans, bring them to the house and pour them out in the middle of the floor, go back and fill them sacks up again. There'd be a big heap, maybe reach from here to way over there, about this high. *(He reached his arm way out and up, to indicate a*

Leland Noble, Robert Turner, Michael Cole, and who else?

huge pile.) Then maybe a couple of families would come and they'd either have a bean stringin' or a bean shellin'. Lots of people shelled out the beans, back then, for soup beans. Whichever house that took place, they'd send somebody down here to Rob's, to the little old country store, you know, to get a quarter's worth of sugar. And one of the women would make candy. So the candy would be done by the time the beans were all worked up.

Where did you go to school?

I went to school at . . . back then it was called Beech, there where you all had church, first off. We walked to school. I remember we were allowed to get one pair of shoes a year. And we could pick out a pair of them, what we called back then, gum boots, or we could get a pair of shoes. And I remember a lot of times we would start up the creek to school, and up there at Levi's where there was this slate rock in the creek—it kinda went up, it went up three or four feet, back then. And those mornings, back then, could get so cold, and

New Moon Over Slick Rock Hollow

that moisture on the ground would freeze and form a great big thick ice on those rocks. We'd have to get down and crawl up those slick slate falls—you couldn't walk it.

There was one stove right in the middle of the schoolhouse. And of course, everybody in the eight grades crowded in there and that created some body heat. And see, you kept your coat on and everything. We didn't go to school that much. Lots of times necessity required that they had to be home to work.

There was no church house. The schoolhouse was the church house. Down here at Crockettsville, Sammy Vandemere, you heard of him? He used to ride a horse down here for meetings and Sunday School. And my parents taught us what was right and wrong; to treat other people like you wanted to be treated, and to be fair. That's something that isn't taught now.

Willie Johnson was born in 1928, to Harlan and Mary (Combs) Johnson. With his eight siblings and parents, he lived up a rugged hollow off Bowlings Creek, just above Slick Rock Hollow. Times were hard, very hard, so in 1938 Harlan moved his family to southern Ohio, close to Miamisburg. The family "made good" in Ohio, but they never forgot their native Kentucky. The boys often came back to visit. Wesley developed close friendships with the Johnson boys. As Willie said, "Wesley and I had an "understanding."

This special interview took place at the Crockettsville Cemetery Memorial Meeting in the summer of 2004.

Seasons of Home
by Woodrow Deaton

I was born August 24, 1920, to Brant and Sally Deaton, at the Rock House Fork of Bowlings Creek, in a house sitting right in the Forks of that creek.

I can't imagine raising a big family in that narrow hollow, with animals and gardens and fields . . .

Our garden was in the "bottom" behind the house right against the foot of the hill, where that point comes down. Our crops were those hillside fields. Ninety percent of what we had, we grew. The only thing they bought was flour, sugar, salt, and coffee. We had our own cornmeal. We'd go to the mill every Saturday and have our meal ground. We had two cows and we butchered our own meat.

Mother cooked all kinds of produce we raised. She would can and dry beans and make kraut. We raised sweet potatoes and produced our own Irish potatoes. Did you ever eat any smoked apples? We had a big apple orchard. We could get apples off the trees, Martha, starting in June, right on up to December. We had two or three or four Black Ben Davis trees. They had big black red, dark apples, about that big. (*Here he indicated a huge apple with his hands.*) Right about this time of year we would go and pick those off the trees. One of us would go up in the tree and the other would hold a big blanket. We would shake the apples out of the trees into that blanket so they wouldn't bruise. Our old house set about four feet off the ground, on one end. We went under the floor and dug a big hole and put those apples in that hole to store them all winter. We stored our potatoes that way too.

There were eight boys and two girls in our family. My Dad and Mother had ten boys and three girls. Two little boys and one little girl died young. I'm the youngest one. I'm number thirteen! Back then, big families were an asset. Most lived on subsistent farms. They grew and raised everything they ate. So you see, the more children they had, the more work hands they had. But, the more mouths they had to feed, too!

My Mother would do her laundry every Thursday. One of my jobs was to carry water. Every Thursday before I went to school, I would fill two #2 tubs full of water (from the well). And I'd fill the **big** round black kettle full of water and build a fire under the kettle.

She did her laundry on a rub board. When I came home that evening, she'd have two big lines of clothes, as far as from here to the street, hanging out to dry. Sometimes in the wintertime, they'd dry stiff as a board, stiff as a rock.

Mother bought cloth from Sears and Roebuck for five or ten cents a yard. She made our shirts and her dresses, on an old pedal sewing machine. And she knit our socks.

I don't know how my Mother cooked for all of us, when we were all at home. She had an old cast iron four-cap step stove. You know what I'm talking about? In other words, the fire box was like, here, and it came back about this far and the oven was in the back, see. The way it was made, the heat would go all around that oven. She cooked with wood. We'd go into the hills and cut the wood and haul it out, saw it up into logs and split it with an ax. We never heard of a chain saw. I'm talking about an old regular cross cut, two-man saw.

We had 30 some, odd head of sheep. We started out with one little ewe lamb that my Daddy bought for me and I carried it home in my arms. That little lamb grew to 30 head of sheep. The sheep grazed on sparse pastures on rocky hillsides, in the summer. In winter they ate soy bean hay. We grew the soy beans in the little creek bottom; just a little level ground. The biggest level field we had was about an acre and a half. We cut the soy beans with a mowing blade.

We would shear those sheep every May and send the wool to Trans Valley Woolen Mills in Virginia. They would clean the wool, spin it and send blankets to us. They would keep half the wool and send us the other half in blankets. Some were blue, some gray, some white—just different colors.

Even though I was the youngest, I had to work awful hard. Yes, sir, I've gone into the fields many a time, when I was a little fellow, Martha, and worked barefooted in the spring and summer, with the mules.

My Daddy would rotate his crops. To start out the crop season, along in January every year, we would have to go and cut the briars and sprouts. Then along in March we'd start plowing. About the middle of April we'd start planting our corn. Then about the first of May, we'd start cultivating. My Daddy would cultivate his corn about three times. Along about the first week in July, we'd have our corn "laid by" (the final cultivating). From there on we'd start harvesting. Before the first big frost, we'd harvest our pumpkins and cushaws and put them inside the corn fodder shocks to keep them from freezing. We had no cash crops whatsoever. My Daddy grew a little tobacco, but just for his own use.

  Years ago, we raised oats. We cut them with a cradle and lay them in wind rows up and down the hill. After it was cured good, we would tie it up in bundles. My brother Sam was tying up oats one day. He picked up a bundle and felt something move. Well, he had picked up a two and one-half foot rattler, lying right across his arms! Another time . . . Sometimes when we got tired we would sit down to rest while working in the fields. You couldn't sit comfortable on the hillside, so we'd dig out a little place to sit in, you know, like a little duck's nest. Well, we were out working and needed a rest. Sam fixed a "duck's nest." When he sat down, he felt something move under him. He got up and looked, and there was a copperhead! He must have been a good fellow because neither one of those snakes bit him. The Lord sure protected him there.

  Once when I was in high school, some of us got together and went to a little church. Somebody said they were having a revival and they had snakes. So we went. When we got there, up on the platform was a box about this big. I didn't know what was in there. We sat in the back and after a while I looked up there and some guy was up there holding a big rattler, about three or four feet long. He was holding it right over his head, walking back and forth across that platform. When he did that I moved back close to the door, because I thought if he turns that thing loose, I'm getting out of here!

  My Daddy, for years, sold "Sayman" products. He also sold fruit trees from Stark Brothers Nursery. He did that in late fall and winter until early spring. He went door to door, up the hill and down the hollow. He had two pair of saddle bags that he filled with Sayman products and put on his mule. He would be gone three or four days, but he came back with empty saddle bags. Sayman products included patent medicines, liniments, salve, soap, bath powders, and pie fillings. That helped a lot, to provide a little income.

In spite of being raised up Rock House, you and your siblings obviously were well educated and had a strong work ethic. How was that?

When Mother was a child, she went to school one day in her life, Martha. She had to walk three miles. She came back that first day and announced, "I'm never going back." She never did. Much later in her life, my oldest brother taught her how to read, after he learned. My Daddy went through the 5th grade. They always told us, "You go to school and get an education and you won't have to work like we did."

All of us went to school at the Bowlings Creek one-room schoolhouse, for our elementary education. All seven of my brothers went to Berea School, close to Richmond, Kentucky. Some went to high school there. Jim went through college there. See, you could work your way through, then. All you had to do, if you could find enough money to pay your fare to Berea, you could get all the way through college and it didn't cost you a dime. They would work half a day and go to school half day. Berea was 50 miles away so the student seldom got back home. That was the only chance they had to go to school beyond grade school. They didn't have a county high school back then. Breathitt High School hadn't even started. That was back in the 20's. The only high schools were church schools: Highland, Riverside, Mount Carmel, Buckhorn (boarding schools).

There were no established churches. The closest one was over at Altro. But my Daddy read the Bible nearly every day. Most of the men who called themselves preachers . . . about the only thing they could do was get up and quote verses from the Bible. They could hardly read and didn't know the meaning of what they were reading. There were two really knowledgeable preachers that I remember. One was Ike Gabbard from Cow Creek in Owsley County. Another one was Luther Johnson who lived near Buckhorn.

What did you do for recreation?

What we did, this is kinda the work schedule my Daddy followed, we would work five days a week in the fields, and on Saturday morning we would work our gardens out, what needed doing there. After that, we would knock off for the weekend. Then we were free to do what we wanted. We didn't have no church or Sunday School to go to, but on Sundays, most always, a lot of people came to my Dad and Mother's place to visit. We children would play marbles, or pitch horseshoes and play ball, whatever. That was our recreation. I remember one time there were 31 people (besides family), who ate Sunday dinner at my Daddy's table. The women helped my Mother cook dinner.

Thanksgiving Day was usually when we would butcher our hogs. Christmas Day was special because we didn't do extra work and because Mother fixed a good big dinner. Her specialty was peppermint pie. Ever eat peppermint pie? She would take a stick of peppermint candy and melt it and make a pie. You could get a **big** stick for about a quarter, back then.

What was transportation like when you were a child?

Walking. Horseback. Wagon. That was it! Until 1933 the **only** road was in the creek, all the way from the Head to the Mouth. There the road ended at the River. The walking path was mostly at the edge of the creek. In 1933 the WPA built a gravel road from the mouth of Duff Fork to the mouth of Canoe Hollow. My Daddy was the foreman of that project. In 1932, after President Roosevelt was inaugurated, there were several government projects initiated: NYA (National Youth Administration), WPA (Works Progress Administration), CCC (Civilian Conservation Corps).

We had no electricity or plumbing. The only water was from a hand dug well. In 1930 we had an awful drought and our well went dry. I carried water from my Uncle's place, about one-fourth mile. Every morning, on the way to school, I took two eight-pound lard buckets, and on the way home I stopped to fill those water buckets and carried them home.

Because of the drought, they had to dig our well deeper, down to 33 feet, through sandstone rock. My brother and brother-in-law did the work. My Daddy put them down in the well in a big square box, fastened to a chain. The chain was fixed to a big bar. He'd let them up and down with a big windlass. They used that box to haul the rock up. He'd dump the rock out and let it down so the boys could fill it again. Finally they hit water. But before that at one point they hit gas, natural gas. They would drill holes for dynamite and blast the rock in the well. One time they thought they heard something down there, sounded like a kettle boiling. They looked down in there and the whole bottom of the well was on fire. They had hit a natural gas well! It burned for a long time—several weeks. Finally they got it put out. That was dangerous, so after that Daddy got a blacksmith blower. They hooked a long pipe to it and blew fresh air down there all the time, so my brothers could go back down and work.

Once a year we cleaned out that well. One time we could hear the water bubbling from the gas, away out to the creek. They decided they better test the well before my brothers went down in there to clean. We tied a carbide lamp to the well chain. You know what a carbide lamp is? My cousin, Floyd Raleigh, was holding the chain. He put a bucket with the lamp, down in there. It hadn't more then cleared the top of the well and the gas ignited. It spurted about twenty feet right up into the air. When that happened, we were all scared and took off running. Floyd dropped that lamp into the well and it sounded about like two dynamites went off! It blew that lamp right out.

Until 1928 the closest post office was at Altro, five miles away. You either walked or rode horseback. The first Beech post office was at the mouth of Curl Tree. George Johnson's wife, Mary, was the first post mistress. When she died, the post office was moved to the mouth of Rock House. It's been in three or four different places. Those government establishments were just in a corner of a little old store. When my sister Aggie had it, they partitioned off a little closet-like room in the house.

Why the name, "Beech?"

When my uncle applied for a post office, the postal department told him to suggest three names. He chose Beech and Poplar and I forget the other one. The postal department selected Beech–B, double e, ch.

All those little creeks (branches) off Bowlings Creek had a name: Rock House, Duff Fork, Curl Tree, Horse Holler, Mud Hole Hollow, Mill Holler, Canoe, Slick Rock, Gay Hollow. I was talking with your mail carrier a few years ago and he said he had 56 mail boxes on Bowlings Creek. When I lived on that creek, there were larger and fewer families. Old man, Craig Combs, had a huge family and owned everything from the Curl Tree all the way to the River.

Will you tell us about your courtship days? (At this point Woodrow's eyes lit up!)

The first time I remember seeing Edna was just a few days before Christmas in 1940. My brother, Sam P., had married a girl from Millers Branch (at Barwick) and was teaching school there. I had gone over there to visit them. On the way back I was riding a mule up Millers Branch to cross that mountain to the head of Bushes Branch. I met Edna walking. She had been up the creek and was heading back down. We met on a little walking path, you know. Well, somebody had to get out of the road because it wasn't wide enough to pass. We looked at each other a minute and she finally stepped out of the road. So I spoke to her and she spoke to me. Sometime that spring I decided to write her a letter. She was a pretty nice looking little girl, you know, and I thought I should get better acquainted with her. Edna was 15 and I was 20. We married in 1943, on November six. The night before we got married, I spent the night at her Daddy's. The next morning we walked a mile down to the railroad station at 5:00 in the morning, to catch the passenger train. Edna and I rode the train to Hazard. Her Daddy and sister went with us. She had to have plenty of chaperones, you know! We got married in Hazard at the USO club building and rode the train back home that evening. I was in the army at the time, and had a seven day furlough. We married on a Saturday and I left for the service the following Tuesday. Edna cried for weeks.

I remember my older sister, Armine. She had a big family— 16 children. She was a praying woman. The last night I ever stayed with Armine (she lived there on Bushes Branch) I stayed all night with Armine, and Martha, when I went to sleep that night, I could hear Armine praying in the other room. When I woke up the next morning, Armine was a prayin' in the other room. She was a mighty mighty deeply religious woman.

Not long ago I walked back up to the Old Home Place on Rock House. The only thing that was left was two gate posts going up to what we called the barn loft. Everything else is gone—the home, the barn, all the other out buildings, everything. The hills were all grown up—gone back to nature.

I interviewed Uncle Woodrow, as Beverlie Riley calls him, in October of 2004, in his beautiful home in Lexington, Kentucky. His gracious wife, Edna (Mosley), was there also. At that time she was confined to a wheelchair. Bev and Rosie were with me. Woodrow's keen mind remembered dates and names and events, precisely.

Mother's Helper
by Elsie Raleigh Johnson

I started school at Wolf Creek, at the Figger Beech School. But just as quick as it started getting cold weather, my legs broke out with sores and they let me quit school. Then we moved to Lick Branch and I went to school there.

Why was it called "Figger Beech?"

There were so many large beech trees all over that hill. There was a big beech tree right at the edge of the cemetery. It was as big around as a big flour barrel. There were letters and "figgers" (figures) cut in that tree where children would take their knives and cut initials and love messages. They just cut that Figger Beech tree down not too many years ago. It was a very old tree. What schooling I got, was at Lick Branch. I got to fifth grade. Back then, children learned at school, if they wanted to. I had to quit school and stay home and help Mother with her babies. We had another little brother. I didn't want him but we got him anyway!

When I went to school we had to walk and skim around the bank and wade the creek in places. And you know, back then, we only got one pair of shoes a year. And if our shoes wore out before warm weather came, we just had to go barefooted. And the way we had to wade that creek, one pair of shoes wouldn't last us all winter.

I study about how we could keep warm back then. We always had to scrounge around for wood to burn for heat and for cooking. The boys cut lots of wood to keep two fireplaces going. The old chimney had a fireplace on each side. And our old houses were cold—open places everywhere. But we wore more clothes then they do now. We wore flannels when we could get it. Mother would make our petticoats out of flannel and we had long leg bloomers. And we wore long stockings. My stockings came up to my bloomers. Our dresses came down to the calf of our legs, just like old women wore. I wore long sleeved petticoats and long sleeved dresses.

When we were children, there would be three or four of us asleep in one bed. I guess that was necessary, to stay warm. Mother would throw four or five homemade quilts over us. I always had to sleep with the little ones. I would sleep with the big baby when Mother had a new little baby. The three big boys would sleep in the other room.

Did you do anything special at Christmas?

No. Well, it was a little extra than any other day. But really, Martha, at that time we didn't know the meaning of Christmas. Mother would always try to manage to get us a mess of fresh meat somewhere. And she'd bake sweet potatoes and she'd make gingerbreads. That was our main treat for Christmas. Earlier she would make those gingerbreads (like big cookies) with sorghum molasses. She would put them in buckets and put lids on them, and hang them up in the kitchen. Our old kitchen didn't even have a ceiling. But it had strips across and she had nails drove up to hang things on, to get it up out of the children's reach. She'd save back a bucket or two of gingerbreads for Christmas.

I don't know how she managed to save that flour because we often just had cornmeal. We had corn bread for breakfast instead of biscuits. And we would usually have fresh churned butter and fried 'taters. We had a big old apple tree and in the summertime we had fried apples for breakfast. We were livin' on top then! We had a big cane patch and in the fall we'd make enough sorghum molasses to do us all winter. Mother would can all kinds of stuff, in big gallon jars, and make sauerkraut in big old crocks. And she'd smoke apples with sulfur. That sulfur would about choke you to death if you'd get a puff of it. We always had big gardens and the boys would raise big fields of corn. We kept a cow or two, and would fatten from one to three big hogs. We kept a big gang of chickens.

My Daddy stayed gone a lot. He'd work for his people some and they would pay him in potatoes or shucky beans or home-killed meat. His sister, Aggie, would make the awfullest lot of butter. She would put that butter out in bowls and sometimes Daddy would bring us a whole basket full of those bowls of butter. We went after that like it was so special. Mother would churn every day or two, but that butter would be eaten up, that first mess.

Mother had to make the most of our clothing. She made the boys' shirts and our dresses. She would save up eggs and take them to a little store to trade for cloth. She had an old Singer treadle sewing machine. We would catch her gone—me and Luther. He would help me get that sewing machine hooked up, when Mother was gone. I wanted to learn how to sew and she wouldn't let me. She was afraid we'd mess it up or break her needles. We'd sew up a storm while she was gone!

I remember one time we had a cow. She was real hateful. She'd kick and pour the milk out. I was wanting to learn how to milk and Mother wouldn't let me. My job was babysitting and dish washing and things like that. That night I got my dishes done early and I sneaked out and went to the barn to milk. I was determined to learn. Well, I had gotten a pretty good bucket full and that cow just picked her old foot up and set it on top of the bucket and turned it over and threw it down. About that time, here came Mother to the barn to milk. "Well, Honey," she said, "you will have no milk tomorrow, for your sneaking out and doing things you know you shouldn't do." But the next day when everybody else had milk, she relented. She made the boys share with me.

My brother Kale was always full of mischief. If he was wanting Mother to kill and fix a chicken and she would put him off, he'd catch one and wring its neck. Then he would hang it in the palin' (wooden fence) and let out hollering every breath, "Mammy, there's an old hen hung in the fence!" It would be dead by the time she'd get to it. So Mother would put on water and heat it and scald the hen and fry it. We had chicken real often just from Kale hanging them on the fence. Brother Luther began to notice what he was doing and said, "You'll keep on 'til we won't have no chickens left to lay eggs."

"Chickens is much better eatin' then eggs, anyway," he said.

Tommy got a call from the army. He caught the measles while he was gone and brought them in on all of us. While Mother had the measles, she gave birth to Leonard. He was early and small and broke out with the measles. He was just a little red bumpy thing, all over.

How many were in your family?
There were just nine boys, and me and Faye, and my half-sister, Polly. Mother lost a set of twins after we moved to the River, and they were both boys. She was about six months along, I think. What brought on her premature labor was. . . . We had just moved to the River and my brothers were learning to cross the river in a boat. They used a pole. Luther was a great big little boy, and one day he fell out of the boat and into the river. Mother was standing on the bank and saw it happen. She knew he couldn't swim and she got scared to death. My Daddy swam out and brought him in, but Mother went into hysterics. She was screaming and praying and going on. Luther was fine, but soon after that she had a miscarriage and lost those twin babies. That was her second set of twins. Ray and Faye are also twins.

Mother had all 13 of her babies at home and a midwife with all of them. Dulcenie Deaton was the one who delivered those twins. That was a scary time for me, because I was just a child and didn't know anything about those things. I knew Mother wasn't feeling well and had lain in bed most of the day. But she got up and fixed an early supper and sent Daddy to fetch the midwife. Well, before he got back with Dulcenie and Aunt Mary (Grandma), Mother, with Luther's help, had already delivered one baby. It was dead. When Dulcenie came, she helped deliver the other one. It was dead too. Two little boys.

After it was all over, Luther went and caught a chicken out of a tree, where they were roosting. I helped pluck it and he cooked it and fixed breakfast, long before daylight. It was the custom to cook a chicken for the midwife before she went on home (I guess as part of her pay). That woman sat there and ate and ate and bragged on Luther's cooking. We had been told there was a little dog in her satchel. Its job was to catch the baby. When she put her dog back in her satchel it was time to cook a chicken and then take the Old Woman back home.

Angeline Spicer was a midwife and I remember one time when she came to deliver one of Mother's babies, she sat and told us tales about her poodle dogs. She said she couldn't catch all these babies if anything happened to her dog. I asked her why she didn't get rid of her poodle dog—people didn't need so many babies! I didn't want all them babies. I had to take care of them. I remember when Mother had her first set of twins, Faye and Ray. I wanted to put Ray in the well. I didn't want him at all. I told the midwife, "We'll keep the little sister, but we didn't need another brother."

Aunt Lizzie said, "We'll not throw it in the well, I'll take it home with me." But they got me persuaded to keep both of them. After all, there weren't many people had twins.

Those little twins that died—they put those little babies in a shoebox that night and set them up on a quilt shelf, on the top shelf. Me and Aunt Mary sat there and watched them all night, 'cause we had old cats, you know. That old cat came in and tried to get up there a time or two, but Aunt Mary (Grandma) would take her old stick and slap it and make it go back out. They took those babies to Wolf Creek the next day. Seems like, the best I can remember, they made a little wooden box and dug a hole and buried them at the cemetery. But, Martha, they looked just like two little dolls laying there in that shoebox. They were the last babies that came to our house. That made 13.

Now you know, back then, there were no churches or Sunday Schools. Every once in a while, some "Holiness" people would come in from other places to the (abandoned coal) camps, to have meetings. Mother would take us children and go, every time she could. But my Daddy wouldn't go, he didn't believe in "Holiness." He ridiculed our Mother. When he drank he would get mean and make life miserable. You talk about a hard life for Mother. But Martha, she would get in such a hard place and she would get down and cry and pray, sometimes at night for an hour. And you know, somebody

New Moon Over Slick Rock Hollow 71

would come that very day and bring us a load of stuff. I know God answered her prayers. And Mommy would go to them Holiness meetings, and we didn't understand it then, but I'm telling you, she'd go and she would get the best blessings! She'd get blessed and she would just get so happy, even after we'd get back home. She would tell the Old Man about it and he would make her hush. He didn't want to hear about it. She said, "Jim, they don't pour nothing on you, it's the Spirit of the Lord!"

I didn't know anything about it, Martha, until I got to feeling it myself. Honey, that's the best feeling you'll ever have in this old body.

Well, when I got older, brother Cale married Effie. I spent time with them and got acquainted with Effie's brother Wilson. Wilson and his sister, Isobel, came and spent the night with us and the next day we went to town together, me and Wilson, on the train. We ran around in town all day and that was the first time we dated. Well, from that, we dated around about two years. Wilson went on to Newport and got a job. One day he sent me a message, "Let's get married." Well, I knew my Daddy wouldn't let me get married and I hated to leave Mother. But I went ahead with our secret plans. Wilson came to Jackson to meet me. The only way I could get away was to go to my Grandpa Raleigh's on Wolf Creek, on a Saturday evening, and stay all night. I told Mother we might not come back tomorrow. If not, I'll be back Monday sometime. Monday was a bad time to plant corn and that is how I got away. We planted by the almanac signs and the signs weren't right. If it had been a good time to work, I would have had to stay home and cook.

I took little brother Leonard with me to keep my parents from knowing anything about my plans. Me and my cousin, Pearlie, went to town that morning. I met Wilson in Jackson. I was kinda afraid to go with him, but I knew if I went back home after he came, that I'd never get away from home no more for nothing. So I went with him to Newport and we got married. I sent little Leonard home on the train with Pearlie and Uncle Elliott's Blanche. When they got home, Mother said, "Where's Elsie?"

Blanche was almost afraid to tell them. "She met Wilson in Jackson and she went to Newport with him to get married." Mother let out a crying and goin' on, you know. Daddy let her cry a few minutes and said, "Dry that up, Old Woman. That's enough. She's older then you was when you got married!"

We married on April 16, and on June 22 Wilson got laid off and we came back home to Breathitt County. Mother and Daddy both were tickled for me to come back.

I remember when I was a great big little girl, long before I married; I started in to Sunday School. We had just moved all our stuff on a sled and mule from Lick Branch to a house on the River at Altro. When we got to our "new" home, there were three of the Bowling children to meet us. Their Mother, Armine, made for me the first doll I ever had, and sent it to me. A big old rag doll, as big as a great big baby. I kept that for years. I was playing with it outside one evening and left it in the corn sled and the hogs got it and tore it up. I cried and I threw a fit over my doll.

Anyhow, I started to go to Sunday School. They were missionaries—Miss Violet, Miss Helen, and Miss Adeline. Later John Haupt married Miss Violet and he was the preacher. They lived up there in one of the section houses, I believe. Well, a whole bunch of us joined them and got saved. We were baptized right there by the mouth of Bushes Branch at the shoals, in the river. A little missionary man from Hazard came and baptized us. There was a big gang—a dozen or more who were baptized. Mother and Armine came and watched us. I was 14 or 15.

I was a Christian then, but it was hard. Some of my brothers made fun of me and sometimes I just quit praying and got discouraged. But one evening Dad took Joe up in the holler to get a load of wood. They cut a tree down and it fell on Joe. It almost killed him. They hollered for me to help get Joe to the house. Back then, the only way out to a doctor or hospital was to go to Hazard on the "up" train or catch the "down" train to Jackson. They took Joe to Hazard. When he came back later that night, he just looked so pitiful, his eyes were crossed.

He looked at me and said, "Elsie, I want you to pray for me." That was so hard, but I was afraid not to pray. I walked over to him and hugged him to me and prayed for him.

My other brother challenged my prayer. He said, "Well, Joe, Christian Elsie prayed for you. You know you have to get better!"

Joe did get better, but his eyes were crossed for a long time. He will tell me, even now, "If it wasn't for you, I wouldn't be here. Your prayer is what saved me."

Elsie is still a praying woman. She prays for her children, grandchildren, and great grandchildren. She prays for her husband and her brothers and sister. I count it a blessing when she prays for me.

Elsie was born on Wolf Creek in 1928 to Jim and Martha Raleigh. They later moved to Big Branch and then to Lick Branch and later to the River at Altro. She and Wilson raised six children. Today, many of the children and grandchildren live close by her home at the Head of Bowlings Creek. Elsie cooks a big meal nearly every day for whoever happens to stop by.

Feb Fork of Gays Creek
by Wesley Stoltzfus

The trail from Gays Creek, up the hollow they call Feb Fork, was as good as any other trail and served its purpose well for many generations. A horse and rider or a mule and wagon could easily maneuver around the rocks and waterfalls and mud holes. Along came trucks and cars and the Feb Fork trail became dreadfully inadequate.

When we write about a community, we need to write about the people, of course. However, the Feb Fork Road, in the fifties, seemed as significant as its people, and certainly more frustrating.

The muddy ruts were "deep enough to bury a mile in," as they say. Actually, that statement wasn't exaggerated too much. In winter we had to pile rocks in both ruts to keep our vehicle from hanging on the middle ridge and our tires from spinning. There were rocky cliffs on the upper side and the slick muddy ridges sloped sharply to the creek bed on the lower side. The Jimmy Smith Hill was formidable! Going down, we would slip slide along erratically and going up was even worse. The dirt (or mud, depending on the season) was scratched out where others had dug in. There were huge rocks leaving barely enough room for a wagon, let alone a 3/4 ton truck. Often the tires would spin out before we reached the top and we had to try again. There was a pole bridge, of sorts, at Luke Begley's, but it was safer to drive in the creek. Working around the cliff was tricky, however!

"Do you believe in angels?" I asked Ethel when I was taking her with her sick child out to Grapevine to see a doctor one day. It was winter and Feb Fork was barely passable. AND, there was a stuck and abandoned car right in the middle of the road! We nearly slid over the bank because I had to, very carefully, ease out of the ruts onto the slick frosty bank. The baby was crying, the mother was scared and I was praying. We made it to the doctor and that baby is still alive today.

We "saw" God's glory many times and His angels protecting us on some very treacherous road conditions.

Once (about 1955) Frank Dutcher, the missionary preacher from Bowlings Creek, drove out Feb Fork in his truck to meet some people from Ohio. These people were in a covered truck, like a U-haul, and were loaded with two huge cast iron furnaces; one for the Bowlings Creek Church and one for the school. A church in Ohio had donated the furnaces and Bill (I think that was his name) and his wife, plus Abe and his wife, brought the furnaces to Gays Creek.

New Moon Over Slick Rock Hollow 75

Frank Dutcher's mules with wagon and visitors—early 1950s.

That was the easy part. The challenging part was getting their loaded truck up Feb Fork and down Bowlings Creek. It was December.

"I think I better drive your truck," Frank told Bill and Abe. "The hill at Jimmy Smith's is bad. I'll drive my truck up first and walk back to take your truck. It's treacherous but I'm familiar with the road."

Abe hesitated, "Uh, no, I better drive the truck. You see, it's borrowed and I feel responsible for it. The road can't be that bad."

So they started out in low low gear; Frank in the lead in his truck. He knew when to stay in the ruts and when not to stay in the ruts. Frank made it to the top of the hill but Abe wasn't so fortunate. Halfway up, at Luke Begley's pole bridge, he became hopelessly stuck. The harder he tried to get out the deeper he dug. Now what? First they piled rocks around the wheels for traction. No help. Next they hitched Frank's truck to Abe's truck and pulled. That only edged Frank's truck dangerously close to the Slick Creek bank! No help there either. It was getting dark and getting colder and there was snow on the ground.

On Feb Fork at the home of Sam and Adeline Spicer.

The only solution to the problem was to get word to me, back home at Bowlings Creek, to come to their rescue. The only ones available to bring the message to me were Bill and his wife and Abe's wife. So they started out walking, on their three and a half mile trek. I hope they had a flashlight because these folks had never been to Bowlings Creek before, and because December nights in Kentucky can be very dark and very cold. At first the trail was in the tire ruts full of icy water, then they had to slosh through the creek bed itself. It was bad. Hours later when they got to our house, they were wet to their knees, with ice hanging from their coats. Some of the details of this episode are blurred in my memory, but I remember well how wet and cold those dear people were.

I drove Frank's logging truck up to the mill. Dock helped me load three or four big logs onto the truck for weight and traction. Then I drove out our hollow and backed down Feb Fork. With another log chain we hitched the logging truck to Frank's truck that was hitched to Abe's truck. We heaved and pulled. Frank's jaws were set. My legs were taunt and shaky and Abe's knuckles were white on the steering wheel. With a final pull and a prayer we got Abe out of his desperate situation. We labored on up the hill and down Bowlings Creek.

Bill spent most of the rest of that night close beside our Warm Morning heating stove trying to get warm.

Back then, Feb Fork was quite heavily populated. Even though the hollow was narrow and deep and only two and one-half miles long, there were about 20-25 families situated along its banks. Large families. Small houses without electricity or plumbing. Strong people struggling to raise their families. Some opted out and moved to points "North."

I recall some of those people.

David Showalter was a Mennonite missionary preacher on Gays Creek. For several months in 1952 I was a volunteer in that community, helping to build a parsonage, teaching, visiting, whatever. In those few months I fell in love with the people on Gays Creek and Feb Fork. Some have become my life-long friends and some will be eternal friends.

One evening David sent John (another volunteer) and I up Feb Fork to "sit up" with Edgar Riley, who was dying of T.B. Back then it was customary, when someone was very sick or dying, for neighbors and friends to congregate at his house, usually all night and many nights. There would be singing and praying and visiting. Sometimes preaching. Always there was lots of black coffee. Mary and her husband, along with several others, were also there at the Riley house. That night I had my first exposure to the practice of speaking in tongues. Mary was a strong seasoned mountain Christian, very vocal. I was a brought on inexperienced young Christian. In that small crowded sick room I had to come to terms with differences in theology. I had to do some adjusting in my thinking about the gift of speaking in tongues.

That night also, I first heard Clifton Riley sing, "Praise the Lord, I Saw the Light," like I have never heard it sung before or since. Down low bass, way way down. A good competition for J.D. Sumner. One could sing, one could speak in tongues, another could give words of encouragement. Together we ministered to a man in his last nights.

Before Clifton got sick, he was one of those "on again, off again" Christians. When he was "on again," he would preach some, and sing, "I Saw the Light." Phil Miller, from Virginia, was our evangelist for revival meetings on Bowlings Creek, about 1967 I think. He and I were visiting some folks on Gays Creek when we stopped at a little country store at the mouth of Johns Fork. Clifton was there, off again, drinking a pop.

"How is it between you and the Lord?" Phil asked Clifton.

"Well, not so good. I'm out of fellowship. I guess I backslid."

"When are you planning to get back in fellowship?"

"I don't know."

"Right now would be a good time, wouldn't it?" Phil pressed the issue.

Immediately Clifton fell on his knees, there beside the pop machine, and began to pray. Seldom have I heard such a penitent prayer. I don't recall but I think Clifton was an "on again" Christian the rest of his life.

I remember Jake Neace, his wife, his children and his grandchildren. Jake had a very painful malady; a hard red crust of eczema on many parts of his thin body. But he meant to serve the Lord. "Whatever the Lord wants me to do, I'll do it."

The Stidhams and the Spicers were also there on Feb Fork. Grandma Adeline was a very good cook and a very good talker. She could make a good meal from one little chicken, talking all the while. Many of the Stidhams and Neaces were part of the Mennonite Church on Gays Creek.

I recall Jed (not his real name). He did some drinking and when he did, he could be difficult. For some reason, the sight of a

New Moon Over Slick Rock Hollow

Hog butchering time on Feb Fork: Wesley Stoltzfus, Ray Smith, and Johnny Nease, November 1962.

church bus rolling down Feb Fork past his house, irked him. For revenge, he threw and smashed a bottle of beer against the side of the bus.

No electricity. No television. No problem. P.R. grew up on Gays Creek, close to the mouth of Feb Fork. He remembers the good times. His parents, Arkansas and Evaline Riley, had a battery operated radio, one of very few in the neighborhood. It was a large shiny console, imposing in their plain front room. Every Saturday night friends and kin gathered at their house to listen to the Grand Ole Opry.

"Us boys would sit on the floor close to the radio so we could hear better," Paul recalls. "There were 20 or 30 people there. Hordes of kids played around outside. Mom had picked several bushels of half-runner beans and everybody joined in the work. Sometimes they would string the beans and break them up, ready for canning. Mom canned hundreds of quarts of beans every year. Her eight sons were hearty eaters! Other times our Saturday night visitors would break the beans in half and string them up for drying under the porch rafters. When dried, those beans were cooked all day with fat pork for delicious shucky beans."

"Those were the good old days."

Today the stream called Feb Fork flows directly into the Buckhorn Lake, a huge reservoir built in 1958 for flood control. Access to the community is from the head of the creek. The Mennonite Church house on Gays Creek, along with dozens of homes, were forced to move out because the lake moved in. Over the years, many persons moved out and many more died out. Generations of people come and go and are soon forgotten.

As for man, his days are as grass or flowers. They flourish, then the wind blows over them and they are gone, and the place remembers it no more. (Psalms 103:15-16)

Sad. Thinking about that could be depressing. But consider this: *From **everlasting** to **everlasting** the Lord's love is with those who fear Him, and his righteousness to children's children.* (Psalms 103:17)

Lord, your faithfulness continues through **all** generations.

– CHAPTER 6 –

Christmas in the Hills

"Where are we? Whose house is that?" It was just after dark, several weeks before Christmas, and Wesley and I were driving home across the hills from town. Around every curve was another bright display of Christmas lights. The lights were dancing and blinking around each door and window so brightly I scarcely recognized the place. We saw several trailer homes, their plainness hidden by thousands of colorful lights. The big house around the next curve had dazzling white icicles hanging from the roof, the porches, the dormers, and the eves. Over there were blue lights chasing each other up and down the porch railing and miles of lighted garlands festooning the fence and porch. Then there was the simple beauty of a house with a single candle at each window, upstairs and down.

"Oh! Look at that!" I squealed. Every bush and tree and window was blazing with tiny lights. Coming down the hill we saw a yard as crowded as the Bethlehem Inn: Mr. and Mrs. Santa and their sleigh with reindeer, elves, nutcrackers, Pooh Bear, candles and candy canes, all illuminated from within. Unlike the Inn, there was room for a plastic Holy Family. Many homes had a beautiful tree inside the window, winking and blinking its Christmas cheer. Up there on the hill was a star and a cross. Up hill and down, for miles, we enjoyed the beauty of Light.

A few hours each day, for several weeks in dark December, the bleak hill-scape is radiant with light. Then, the rainy day after Christmas, most ambitious homeowners are busy untangling yards of lights and storing Santa and his reindeer.

The darkness returns.

There is a Light that has been gleaming from before the creation of all other lights. This Light will never be extinguished and will shine ever brighter into eternity. Jesus is the Light of the world; everyone who follows Him will not walk in darkness, but will have the Light of Life. "For Jesus is now that Star divine, brighter and brighter He will shine."

* * * *

Jessie Banks reminded me that Christmas in the Hills has not always been so gala, full of lights and gifts. "My Mother married at 14 and birthed 13 children," she told me. "She raised 11 of those plus two grandchildren, and cared for both her parents and her mother-in-law until they died. So, celebrating Christmas didn't include spending money, because there wasn't much. However, there was plenty to eat. We cooked and feasted. There was chicken and dumplings, fried chicken and fresh hog meat. There were mashed potatoes and baked sweet potatoes and shucky beans cooked in hog grease. There were several kinds of cakes and we made candy and popcorn balls stuck together with sorghum. There was "tough jack," a kind of hard pull taffy made with sorghum. For decorations we strung popcorn, raised in our garden, and draped it around a straggly cedar tree. For recreation we skated on a water hole by the creek. We had no skates, just our old shoes."

"Life was simpler then."

* * * *

Rosetta Cole Deaton recalls, "Back then, we didn't get a lot of presents, we didn't even know there was all that stuff out there in the world. We were poor and had no money for Christmas. Uncle Jesse and Aunt Ethel lived in Ohio. They had no children, so every year they sent us a Christmas box, with a few little gifts for us children. One year it was little rubber dolls for us girls. We thought them dolls was everything! Every year in that box was some hard candy. We ate on that candy for six months!"

Rosetta has no regrets for her meager Christmases so long ago. She has learned contentment. She told me her Christmas memory story as she lay in her bed at the Jackson Nursing Home. She is blind and tired and her get about ability is limited to occasional wheelchair rides to the dining room and three trips a week by ambulance to Hazard for kidney dialysis. Yet Rosetta is cheerful. Content. One of her friends hesitates to visit her in that situation and environment. "Because," she says, "it's so depressing."

"I'm not depressed." Rosetta smiled and I knew she was speaking the truth.

Rosetta spent her first Christmas in heaven in 2004.

* * * *

Mose Turner recalls:

Christmas! That was the happiest time of my life! Our kind of Christmas then doesn't seem like Christmas now. But, we would always cut a cedar tree, and then we would pop some popcorn and thread it on a string. Then we would make crepe paper chains and run them across the ceilings and decorate that tree with just what we had. For candy, we'd go to a hickory tree and skin some of the bark off and cook that bark and then strain it, you know, keep that liquid and then make candy. It had a real good super taste.

We always thought there was a Santy Clause, but he doesn't come 'til you go to sleep in the night. And I can remember, boys, I'd go to bed at the edge of dark so Santa Clause would hurry up and come. And I'll tell you what, I was out of that bed the crack of daylight. And you know, Mom and Daddy tried to have an apple and an orange and a bar of candy in our stocking. And, Lord, those were the best Christmases. Seems like, then, there was lots of snow at Christmas and those pine trees would just bow down at the edge of dark and it would just put you in such a spirit, such a Christmas spirit.

* * * *

It was a snowy Sunday just after Christmas. Wesley and I drove up the road (very carefully because of the snow) to check on Belle. She was busy sweeping snow and carrying in coal. Wesley carried in more coal for her and put it on the porch. Then we went on to visit Roscoe and Betty.

"Tell me some of your childhood Christmas memories," I coaxed.

Betty recalled, "We knew Christmas was coming when Daddy robbed the bee gums. He had lots of bee gums and he stole enough honey from the bees for our family and for our friends and neighbors. Canning jars filled with comb honey is a pretty sight. And sweet! Mommy would cook and bake for two days—hog meat and fried chicken and several kinds of cakes. Stack cakes and ginger cakes were Christmas specialties. And Daddy would often buy fudge for Christmas. I think it was called Aunt Hetty's fudge. He would get two boxes, one chocolate and one white. There were four big pieces in a row, sixteen pieces in each box."

Then Roscoe began to reminisce: "Christmas Day was just like any other day except we had butchered a hog and we had fresh hog meat and Mammy baked cakes sweetened with sorghum. Back in the summer we raised all that sugar cane; that whole bottom out there was planted in cane. In the fall we made the 'lasses. That was a big job because we filled nine 50-pound lard stands with sorghum molasses. There was a big house full of us—all us young'uns and sometimes some cousins or nephews lived with us for awhile. But we never had to buy any sugar 'cause we sweetened everything with sorghum. Cakes and biscuits with cow butter, even our coffee, was all made sweet with 'lasses.

Now, because of health problems, Betty and Roscoe can't eat cakes or hog meat or honey or molasses. What a pity! But they have the memories that still make a person's mouth water.

* * * *

It seems there were two common events in those "back then" Christmases—the men butchered a hog and the women baked a stack cake.

The Christmas hog had been fattened with corn and confined in a small pen, ready for slaughter. The bigger and fatter, the better. That meant more meat and especially more fat. A 400-pound hog was not unusual. A fire was built under the huge iron kettle in the yard where the operation took place. It was hard work and cold and it took all day, but nobody complained. This was a fun family event. Besides, everybody was hungry for fresh meat.

Apparently Grandma, of necessity, cooked plain food—soup beans, corn bread and 'taters—all winter except on Christmas Day. For the cook, Christmas was the second most important day of the year. The first being Memorial Meeting. Thinking about that old Christmas nearly always brings to mind fresh hog meat, stack cake, and ginger cakes.

While Pap and the boys were butchering, Mammy would "build" the stack cake, so called because she literally stacked it six or seven layers high. The ginger and molasses cake batter was baked in thin layers with spicy cooked dried apples between and on top of the layers. I'm including a recipe, but don't be too disappointed if it doesn't turn out like Mammy's did. I doubt that you have home-grown antique apples or sorghum molasses or even a black bread pan or skillet. Or the time and patience. The technique Mammy used to make the dough was also unique. She made it the way she made her biscuits. No utensils needed except her fingers and the palm of her hand. I'm thinking one important tip for success was this, *Let love flow through your fingers as you mix, pat and mold, by hand.*

Bev describes Grandma Della and her Mother-in-law Evaline, making stack cake: "She had a big dishpan covered with a clean tea towel that was always full of flour. When she wanted to make biscuits or stack cake or gingerbread, or whatever, with her hands she made a 'well' in the flour and poured all the other ingredients (the lard was melted) in that well. Then with her fingers, she deftly mixed the flour into the wet ingredients until she had a ball of dough, just the right consistency. For biscuits, she pinched off small balls with her thumb and forefinger and placed them into her black pan. For stack cake, she patted a thin layer, like a huge pancake, in her skillet and baked them, one layer at a time. It was important to make the cake several days ahead, to give it time to get moist, so all the flavors could blend."

Old Fashioned Stack Cake

(From Beverlie Riley who got it from Creta Rose Amis
who got it from her Mother, who was one of the few persons,
at that time, who had a cookbook.)

4 cups flour	2 eggs, well beaten
2 tsp. baking powder	1 cup butter or shortening
1 1/4 tsp. salt	1 cup buttermilk
2 tsp. ginger	1 cup molasses or brown sugar
1 tsp. soda	

Sift flour; add eggs, baking powder, salt, soda, ginger, sugar, molasses, shortening, and milk. Make a stiff dough. Do not roll, just pat in layers into 9 inch layer pans and bake at 375 degrees for about

20 minutes. Makes 6 or 7 thin layers. Spread each layer with apple butter, applesauce, or dried apples (cooked, sweetened, and spiced). This cake is better if allowed to cool and set a day or two before serving.

* * * *

Twas the night before Christmas, and all through the house,
Not a creature was stirring, not even a mouse.

One day, just before Christmas, the church women were busy making star tray favors for the hospital and the nursing home. We were all working at Maxine's long extended dining table and chatting. "Patty," Mary said, "tell us about a special childhood Christmas memory you have."

Well, Patty started in on that "Night before Christmas" poem and recited it without a hitch, all the way to "Merry Christmas to all, and to all a good night."

Then she said, "Every year at our Christmas Program at Altro School, Mose made me say that poem. Nobody else would do it. That first time, he sent word to me, said he wanted to see me in his office. I was scared to death. I thought sure I was in trouble. You see, me and my girlfriend had got in the habit of smoking. One day I would bring a cigarette and the next day she would bring one and we would share it. I thought we had been found out and Mose would whup us! (There are so many Mr. Turners in the school system that the students used the teacher's first name, at least outside the class room.) I was purely shaking when I walked into his room. But all he wanted was to ask me to say that poem for the program. I told him I would. I figured that was better than taking a whupping."

Patty has long since quit school and quit smoking, but she always agrees to recite that poem at our yearly New Year's Eve celebration at the church.

* * * *

Beverlie Riley shared this story.

"When I think of Christmases past, I remember the little red mittens. But to understand who gave me the mittens, I must tell this story."

Back in the forties or the fifties, somewhere in south Ohio, lived a young man with a wife and two small children. One day this young man disappeared—totally. He left no clue as to his whereabouts. His wife never found him. Years passed and he was assumed dead. He wasn't dead. He escaped Ohio (from what or why I don't know) and came to Breathitt County in Eastern Kentucky, to Bushes Branch of the North Fork. There he settled and married Lucy Neace. She died less then a year after their marriage. (She is buried at the tiny cemetery at the head of Bushes Branch and every year on Memorial Day I place some flowers on her grave.)

Then he married young Armine Deaton. Together they raised a large family and Armine didn't know that her husband had a wife and children back in Ohio. His name was Johnny Bowling and he was my grandfather. He was a preacher. (Belle said he was the one who baptized her.)

Years later, when that young man was an old man, several of his sons on Bushes Branch heard some clues about their half-brothers, and went to Ohio looking for them. I don't know how my Grandfather felt about it, but his long lost children were found. So, my Grandfather's two children in Ohio and his eight children in Kentucky got acquainted and established some kinship. The past was forgiven and forgotten, I guess. I have not forgotten the red mittens.

One Christmas when I was perhaps 8 years old, my uncle from Ohio, the one we hadn't known existed, came to visit his relatives on Bushes Branch. As a Christmas gift, he brought me a pair of red mittens and a pair of boots. Even though I walked half a mile to and from school in mud and snow and rain and cold, I had never had mittens or boots. Perhaps for him the gift said, "We can't help for the conduct of our parents. We are family." For me, the gift was warm and dry feet and hands.

My parents divorced soon after I was born, so Mother's parents raised me. However, I spent lots of time with my other grandparents, Johnny and Armine Bowling, who lived just down the creek. Armine was a very Godly woman. She was no doubt the most important Christian influence in my young life. I remember her prayers.

She gave birth to a whole passel of children and then had another girl. That child was very sweet, and smart. She was everything a little girl should be and we all called her Sissy. One day Grandma was carrying a bucket of boiling water to do the washing. Sissy came running to her mother, all excited. They collided and the scalding water dashed all over Sissy. After that, she was a total invalid, both in body and mind. Grandma had to live with consequences of that accident the rest of her life.

What does that story have to do with Christmas? Well, after Sissy's accident, she spent weeks at a children's hospital in Louisville. I think it was Louisville. When she returned home, some organization at the hospital sent a Christmas gift to Sissy every year. Sissy didn't have the capacity to see or know the gifts so Grandma Bowling would wrap up the gift in brown paper and put my name on it. Then she instructed her son (my uncle who was only a little older than me), "When you go to school today, place this gift under the Christmas tree at school. I want little Beverlie to have it." One year it was a coloring book with some water colors and a paint brush. Another time it was twin dolls, each wrapped in a blanket. Such is the love of a grandmother.

And such is the love of God. Regardless of our ancestors or descendents, our personal lives are in the hands of an all knowing God who weaves everything together for our good. That is security!

* * * *

Christmas Carols

We were warming up and relaxing in the church fellowship room (more commonly called The Basement), after several hours of Christmas caroling in the community. The year was 2000. Children were scurrying around like so many church mice, snatching cookies and chocolates from platters on the table. Melody removed her cap, sending her tousled curls in every direction. Little Brian slid off Rocky's shoulders where he had been riding, safe from all real or imagined dogs. Paul checked the coffee pot, ready for a black caffeine boost. Daddy Lloyd was stretching his arthritic back. We were a motley, intergenerational (ages 5 through 80) crew, but we had been doing what we sang: "Go, tell it on the mountains, that Jesus Christ is born!"

Rhonda handed me a cup of hot cider. "I think you'll like this," she said.

This is absolutely my favorite Christmas tradition, I thought, *caroling.* My mind went back to past experiences of Christmas caroling. Many years ago.

When I was a girl, I eagerly anticipated my 16th birthday. After that, I was considered old enough to be part of the church's youth group and to participate in all the youth activities. For me, the most exciting activity of the year was the nearly all night carol singing from an open truck on Christmas Eve. At about 9:00 p.m., 30 or 40 young people would gather at Glick's Plant Farm. We all climbed into Smoker's open grain truck. He had placed plenty of straw in the bed, so it was like a winter hayride.

December winter nights are cold in Pennsylvania, sometimes very cold. We dressed for the occasion. My sisters and I would rummage in all our drawers to find enough long underwear, heavy stockings, sweaters, jackets, scarves, and mittens. Pants were taboo for us girls so we resorted to pajamas under our dresses! In addition to all that, each of us carried a warm quilt for a snuggler between stops.

Finally we were off, the snow crunching under the wheels of the truck. One of the Kauffman's rode in the cab. He had a big flashlight and helped direct the driver in and out of lanes and driveways and pastures. For the next three or four hours we drove all over our part of Lancaster County, for many miles, singing carols for the sick, the old, the needy, and the preachers.

> *Christmas time! Happy time!*
> *All our sins and sorrows should be put away*
> *And we should sing, Hallelujah!*

Some lived in villages, many on farms and other out of the way places. "That young Amish farmer way down below Gap had a bad accident, he needs our songs," Bud Kauffman said.

"Joy to the World, the LORD is come!" We sang as we slowly rode through Smoketown, Monterey, Kinzers, Ronks, and Cross Keys. The men at the tavern at Smoketown stepped out on the porch to listen,

> *Oh, come let us adore Him.*
> *Christ the Lord.*

One year it snowed. We just batted the snow off our eyelashes and dusted it off our heads and kept on singing. Once the skies were so clear and the stars so close, I thought I saw the angels when we sang,

> *Angels from the realms of glory, wing your flight ore all the earth.*
> *Ye who sang creation's story, now proclaim Messiah's birth.*

Over and over we sang, "Oh Beautiful Star of Bethlehem." Some of the girls led out with the melody. The rest of us girls harmonized in alto. Ray Kauffman and Mel Lapp sang tenor and Wesley, Art Kauffman, and Leroy Beiler joined, in their deep bass. I didn't know it then, but I'm sure the four part harmony was beautiful, ringing out in the clear night air.

I thought Dan A.'s Wes had a deeper, stronger bass voice than anybody and I wished he would sit beside me. Sure enough, when we pulled out of Dave Lapp's driveway and were headed toward Stumptown and we settled back into the straw, Wes's quilt was snuggled against mine! Then the stars sang!

After midnight, when we got back home, we were cold and exhausted. Our voices were hoarse and we were hungry. No matter; I wouldn't have missed it for anything. Many of the young people, including Wesley, lived on dairy farms, so they slept only a few hours, then had to get back up at 4 or 5 a.m. to help milk the cows. No matter; they wouldn't have missed it either.

When Wesley and I married and moved to Kentucky, I was thrilled to learn that these little church groups go caroling also. For the past fifty years the little group at the Bowlings Creek Mennonite Church has continued this tradition. In the early years, a very small group, mostly children, ready for the adventure and the hot chocolate and cookies, ventured out at twilight, on foot. Their thin slipons (shoes) soon became wet and muddy as we sloshed through the creek and up the hollers. Their light jackets were little defense against the night chill. Some of their voices were off key and some didn't sing at all. We were having fun, though, and we extended the Christmas message to some lonely people.

> *Away in a Manger, no crib for His bed,*
> *The little Lord Jesus lay down his sweet head.*

Later, with improved roads, we hauled the carolers in a van or two and several cars. Then every able body, young or old, rode along to herald the Christmas message.

New Moon Over Slick Rock Hollow

Joy to the World, the LORD has come.
Let earth receive her King.

At Bobby Johnson's house Marthy pressed her thin face against the window pane to see who was there. Jimmy Deaton subdued the angry dogs at his house and Ida joined in, "Oh come all ye faithful." We had to go early to Levi and Bell's; else they would already be in bed. He would be sitting on the couch by the fire in the grate, a blanket over his thin knees. She stepped out on the porch, enjoying the singing. At Jerry and Eliza's house we sloshed across the bottom field, walked the bridge (not too many at a time!), and jumped across the hollow. If the hollow was "up," we tried to balance on a rock mid-stream. If the rock teetered . . . OOPS! There was always a sturdy bridge at Delbert and Dora's house, and concrete walks to the clean porch.

We drove to the Head of the Creek and around to Gays Creek, stopping to sing for the elderly Turners and Rileys and Smiths, and for Grandpa Blank. He always came out and gave us each a candy bar. We went down Bushes Branch and across the hill to sing "The Drummer Boy" for J.D. Moore. At Lizzie's house Patty cleared the dogs off the porch and Brian scrambled up on Rocky's shoulder, while we sang,

Oh beautiful Star of Bethlehem,
Shining afar through shadows dim.
Giving a light for those who long have gone.

One night we drove up to the house where Crow was living. We trudged up close to the porch singing *"Silent Night, Holy Night, All is calm, all is bright!"* Suddenly the silent night was shattered. "What's going on here?!" Crow ran out from the barn swinging his pistol and hollering. He had been hiding out; to way-lay some rowdies who had been throwing fire crackers into his yard. He was obviously drunk and we had surprised him. When he saw Wesley, he calmed down some but continued to swing his pistol. Carolers stopped singing in mid song and scurried in every direction. We ran for the van and forgot to give Crow his basket of goodies.

"Do you need your cup re-filled?" Rhonda brought me back from my reminiscing, back to the church basement.

"Yes, please," I said and reached for another chocolate candy. It had been another good evening of caroling. Another reason to praise Jesus. This was perhaps my 50th year and I would have hated to miss it. Later, I went to bed, tired, but I couldn't sleep. I was still "high" on Christmas caroling. Besides, I had overdosed on sugar and caffeine, cider and coffee, and chocolate.

* * * *

Carols, Gospel songs and hymns are powerful tools in God's hands. When we participate in singing, or are merely listening, we are confronted with the truth, our emotions are stirred and we are motivated to worship and to action.

Oh Beautiful Star of Bethlehem . . .
Guiding the pilgrim through the night . . .
For the redeemed, the good and blest . . .
For Jesus is now that Star divine.

This gospel song is a favorite for many of us. The lyrics are simple and comforting and the chorus is fun to sing, where the melody singers lead out with, *O beautiful Star,* and everyone else joins in harmony, *beautiful, beautiful star.* Whenever that song is sung, I always remember those long ago all night Christmas hayrides when we were young.

That song is also Paul Riley's favorite birthday song, and Elburn Deaton claimed it wasn't only a Christmas song. One hot

August Sunday morning, he came to church with Paul and Bev. "Tell them to sing Beautiful Star of Bethlehem," he whispered to Bev. So we did. He was an old man and couldn't hear very well, so he sat on the main front bench. But he could hear that song. Tears were streaming down his face and he held his face in his hands and wept when we sang,

> *Beautiful Star, the hope of rest . . .*
> *Yonder in glory when the crown is won.*

Daryl Fyffe recalls that song being sung at his mother's funeral.

* * * *

> *Go! Tell it on the mountains,*
> *That Jesus Christ is born!*

– *CHAPTER 7* –

Mother's Day for Sally

We were just home from church on a Sunday morning. Wesley was placing a bologna and cheese sandwich on the skillet. I was pouring grape juice for the two of us and musing: *I wonder what other Old Mothers eat for Mother's Day lunch when their children are far away? . . . I'm glad I still have an Old Father to share it with. . . . My Mom has been gone over 40 years. . . . She was a woman of very few words, which reminds me of the truth that life's values are caught rather than taught. . . . The service this morning was good, rather emotional since we are leaving for Indiana, and it's Mother's Day. . . .*

My musings were interrupted when Wesley picked up the ringing phone.

"Yes?"

"Wesley, this is Clarence. Come up to the house and eat with us."

"Well, I don't know, I've started some sandwiches."

"Leave those sandwiches. You can eat them another time. We're fixing a big Mother's Day dinner. We're about ready to carry the roasted pig up to the kitchen. We'll be eating in a few minutes. Come on up."

No way could we refuse that invitation. We covered the half-done sandwiches and headed up the hill to Frank Turner's house. What we experienced in the next several hours would seem unreal and extravagant to a foreigner. But for us mountain folk it's just another expression of who we are. On a day by day schedule we cook just enough to get by, but give us a special occasion and we splurge and feast!

New Moon Over Slick Rock Hollow

Cooking had started the day before when the Turner men butchered a 250 pound hog and stuffed it into a pig roaster, fired with charcoal. They had watched and tended that hog all night. Beside the hog cooker was a huge iron kettle full of soup beans and salt pork. The wood fire under the pot kept the beans bubbling and steaming. Early that morning, they had thrown in a wild turkey with the pig. Wesley claimed some credit for that turkey. We had been hearing a gobbler in the hill across the creek. Wesley had called John A.

"You boys lost one of your tame turkeys? No? Well, we are hearing something gobbling." Sure enough, the next day we heard a gun shot and now the tom turkey was part of a Mother's Day celebration.

Frank's daughters had been busy since yesterday, hustling and bustling and cooking and talking. Now they stopped talking long enough to hug us and invite us inside. Half of the hog was laid out on the kitchen table, so tender it needed no carving—just several forks to tear it apart. Every corner and table and counter in the small kitchen was stacked with cakes and puddings and pies. Shirley was putting the finishing touches on an angel food cake garnished with fresh strawberries. Gladys was at the stove fixing the dressing and I don't know what else. Eileen was here, there and everywhere, making everybody laugh. Glenda was loading the dining room table.

Ah! The dining room table! The room was scarcely big enough for the table and the eight foot long table was certainly not long enough for all the food. From edge to edge, the table was literally covered with bowls and platters and cookers, full of Frank's generous offering. Besides the meat and beans, there was chicken and dumplings, potato salad, macaroni salad, other salads, kraut and wieners, pickled beets, sweet potato pie, mashed potatoes, corn bread and light bread, gravy, sweet corn and green beans, every brand of pop you could want plus coffee, and a HUGE Winn Dixie chocolate cake proclaiming, "Happy Mother's Day."

Finally the cooks retreated to the porch for a break and a smoke, while Wesley said the blessin'. "Grab a plate and get something to eat," Frank announced to his three dozen or so guests. Men came first, then everyone else, kids elbowing their way through the crowd to grab a pop and a piece of cake. Fortunately the rain had stopped so when the living room was filled with people struggling to juggle a plate piled high and a can of pop, the guests could spill out onto the porch and yard. Even if you had wanted to, you couldn't get away from the babble of voices. Everyone talked at once, so in order to be heard, each had to talk a little louder. The volume kept going higher.

This was a Mother's Day celebration and Mother Sally was enjoying every minute. She was walking from room to room, outside and inside, smiling and talking, and enjoying her family and friends.

Finally the feasting subsided but not the talking. There were several politicians present so the conversation (when you could decipher it) ranged from local politics to chickens and goats, to gardens and grandkids and everybody's ailments, to who killed who and the weather and who died and who is going to have a baby. Eileen was on the phone, begging everybody she could reach to come to the feast. "There is still lots of food here—half a hog. Come eat with us."

I found Wesley on the porch with a dozen men discussing the rainy weather and how it would affect the gardens. "Let's go home," I said. "It's Mother's Day. My children will be calling me." We did and they did. They rose up and called me "Blessed."

Many mothers had been honored in various ways that Sunday, but I think none had been honored quite as extravagantly as Sally.

– CHAPTER 8 –

Heart Notes

An Ode of Praise for My Fingers

    With my fingers I can mold a biscuit and peel an apple,
    Brush my hair and tie shoe laces.
    I can smooth the sheet on my bed and feel the fuzz on a
        new baby's head.
    With my fingers I can thread a needle
    And crochet an afghan.
    Zip a zipper and fasten a button.
    I give praise that I can turn the pages of a book
    And hold a pen to write these words.
    With my fingers I can turn the knobs on my washer,
    Strike the keys of a computer and dial a phone number.
    When we come home on a cold winter night, I can turn
        the lock to our front door,
    Flip the light switch
    And turn up the thermostat.
    I can pull a weed and pluck a flower.
    With my fingers I can squeeze the water from the mop
    And polish a window.
    Though my fingers are gnarled and my knuckles
        are thick,
    I can pick and snap a basket of beans,
    And later, unscrew the canning jar lid that holds
        the bounty.
    I can hold a hoe, a scissors or a steering wheel.

With my fingers I can clasp your hand and trace the lines
   on your face.
Or erase the tears of a child and watch the smile emerge.
I can open my Bible to read
And entwine my fingers in a gesture of prayer.
I praise you, Creator of my body, for my fingers.
Amen.

Touch the Moment

We have this moment to hold in our hands
And to touch as it slips through our fingers like sand.
Yesterday's gone and tomorrow may never come,
But we have this moment, today.

Those words came to mind this morning. The "moment" was 10:00 Saturday morning. Wesley and I were eating brunch at the picnic table on the patio—pancakes and fried apples and coffee. The air was bright and clear. There were sun and shade patterns on our red checkered tablecloth.

The white and yellow and red colors in my flower beds were brilliant in the morning sun. I saw a rainbow in a blade of dew wet grass. The chickadees were not afraid to join us, at their table. Most of the birds were quiet and resting from their busy summer of raising babies, but I knew they were there.

The coffee was good. The pancakes were good, the telephone wasn't ringing, and Wesley and I were both in good company—each others. People ask us what it's like in the Empty Nest. Wesley says, "It's not empty, the Little Woman and I are there."

I say, "We miss the children, and you may not understand this, but we are having a blast! We enjoy each other."

And this morning I'm thinking how precious this moment is as it slips through our fingers like sand. How much longer will we have each other? Health and life are frail. How much longer will we have this secluded place? It's too far from the children. But this day, this moment, I will cherish.

A Snake Hike

Betty Noble found this picture in Pap's old collection. We don't know who the boy is, but he killed a huge rattler.

It was a perfect evening for a hike. I often walked alone, but this time Wesley joined me. Before we started, he dug out of his pocket, his new pocketknife—the one Steve gave him for his birthday, and cut a long, stout switch from a nearby tree, "just in case."

"Just in case" we meet another snake. Earlier that day, on our way home from the Memorial Meeting at the Combs Cemetery, we had encountered a 42" rattlesnake. Driving up the bank at Delbert Combs' homeplace, we saw that a small car had blocked the road. Two crying babies were in the car. Their mother was wandering around, scared and excited. Two boys, Billy and Bobbie, were throwing rocks. "A snake! A snake!"

"I better get out and help them kill that snake," Wesley said. The back part of the rattler was pinned down by the tire of the car, but it was still very much alive. The babies were still crying and the boys were beating the air with a baseball bat and a club, and were "rocking" the car. Wesley peered under the car to assess the situation. Wham! That monster snake struck and barely missed Wesley's face.

"Look out Wesley! Them things can strike." Billy really got excited.

"Stupid me. We better try something else." He looked around for a very long, very stout stick—like a whip. With all that ammunition, they finally stunned the snake enough to rake it out from under the car and killed it. The mother relaxed and the babies stopped crying. Gleefully, the boys picked up the dead snake by its rattler tail and, running, took it home to show their Daddy.

Now, with a stout switch in hand, we decided to walk up the dry creek bed, for our hike. Never in our nearly 50 years on Bowlings Creek had we seen the creek so dry. During a very dry spell like this is when you have to watch out for rattlers; they come down out of the hills looking for water.

Wesley began to reminisce, "The wagon tracks in the sandstone creek bed were visible for years, but I can't see them anymore. The water has finally washed them away. Or are my eyes just dimmer?! Used to, we would drive down to the river in the creek bed, before there were roads, in a wagon pulled by mules; later with a truck. Navigating "The Falls" at Levi Combs was tricky, but from there to Rob's Lane was easy going; the creek bed was rather smooth. From there to the river was very rough and rocky."

It was a perfect evening for a hike. "Lord," I prayed, "thank you that Wesley and I still have each other, that we can enjoy each other. We can still walk together, after 45 years. Amen."

Finally we turned and walked back to the house. No snakes, thank goodness. Wesley parked his switch by the back door, for future "just in cases."

Lizards and Coffins

I never know what I'll find when I get home from grocery shopping in Jackson. It's nearly as unpredictable as when the children were still at home. All I want is a cup of coffee and a copy of the *Readers Digest*. Wishful thinking, that. Today when I opened the door, I saw the chairs all out of place and Husband kneeling at the back of the refrigerator, with a bug spray gun. "What in the world?"

"Look out! There's a huge rusty joe lizard in here somewhere. He skittered behind the fridge, and I don't know where he is. Wherever he is, he is awful sick." He shook the nearly empty spray can.

We ate our lunch and I thought the sandwich tasted sprayish.

"Come out to the shop with me," Husband invited. "I finished that coffin." He is a craftsman and was filling an order for Harlan.

"Make it of cedar, plain and simple; narrow at both ends like the old timers had. I'll put off needin' it as long as I can, but when it's finished, I'll come and get it. I tell my daughter hit'll be purty enough for a coffee table."

Now it's finished but Husband thought we should try it out before he calls Harlan. So, he helped me climb into the sweet smelling box and I folded my hands over my chest and closed my eyes. "It's plenty big enough for you."

Then it was his turn. It was a snug fit and his belly came almost to the top! And Harlan is nearly as big as he is.

Experiment completed, I sat down with a cup of coffee. It tasted like cedar. I got safely out of the coffin but I'm still looking for the lizard.

Mom's Hands—A Eulogy

Your hands, unadorned, were kissed golden brown by the sun.
Those brown hands

Braided my hair,
Guided cloth through the Singer treadle sewing machine
    to sew our clothes.
Your hands tied the starched strings of my white Sunday
    cap, under my chin.
They mended and folded our brown cotton stockings.
And deftly crimped the edges of crusts of dozens of Shoofly
    pies.
Your hands tended a vegetable garden
And picked luscious strawberries for freezer and friends.
Your hands coaxed flowers into bloom:
Iris and Peonies by the driveway,
Joseph's Coat and Impatients at the shady side of the house,
Poppies and Primroses by the border, Roses on the arbor,
Geraniums in a bed beside the house, and potted Ferns in
    the living room.
Today your hands are cold, folded in death, at rest.
But in a "Land of Pure Delight, where Saints Immortal
    Reign"
Your hands will be lifted in praise, to the Lamb of God, your
    Redeemer!

Sunday Stroll

We should have stayed at home and taken a Sunday afternoon nap, as old people are prone to do. Instead, I tied on my walking shoes and found my walking stick at the back door. Wesley was reading the Sunday School paper. "I think I'll walk up the holler to Curly Head and Mandy's old place, to see what's blooming this week," I informed him. "Are you coming?" He deliberated.

"Naw," he finally said. "I'd like to, but I'm so stiff and tired and my bad ankle is giving me fits. I better save my energy." I started out the door.

"Wait," he said. "How are you getting across the creek?"

"On rocks. I'll be alright if I don't slip and fall." He hoisted his weary body out of his recliner.

"I'll set you across. Give me a few minutes." Soon he rode out of the shed on the Cub Cadet lawn mower. When he removed the mower platform he had his own version of an All Terrain Vehicle—a four wheeler! He rode slowly across the creek with me riding on the back. I jumped off, but instead of riding back to the shed, he started that little tractor up the hollow. He had changed his mind. "I'll go with you."

"It's a little early for the trillium but here is one!" I yelled above the tractor noise.

"Did you ever see so many colors and varieties of violets?" he yelled back.

"I noticed a carpet of violets on our pet cemetery."

It was a balmy day in early April and we were enjoying spring and having fun. I hiked along and Wesley was conserving his energy on the tractor. We ambled along about a quarter of a mile when suddenly the tractor tilted too far into the bank, the wheel lodged between a rock and a hard place, all the air escaped from the tire and our ATV was stuck. The hollow wasn't more than six feet across with a six foot bank on both sides and full of large wet slippery rocks. He shut off the tractor.

"There is no way I can get to the tire, to fix it." He looked a little embarrassed but then he grinned. "It isn't nearly as bad as the times on Bushes Branch or Feb Fork, when the truck wheels would sink in the mud to the axle. You stay by the tractor while I go back and get what I need to get us out of this mess."

So I sat on the bank and waited. Then I dug up some trillium to take home and waited. Finally I saw him stagger up the hollow. He carried two tanks of compressed air on his back and carried a gunny sack with a socket wrench to take off the wheel, a web rope, and a heavy stob. And he was covered with mud from his green John

Deere cap and hair sticking out from under the hat, to his shirt and pants and shoes. Even his glasses were mud spattered. "What happened? Did you fall?"

"Yeah, in that big mud hole."

"Are you hurt?"

"Just my dignity." Then he got to work. With a web rope he anchored the tractor to a tree on the bank. Then he placed the stob under it to jack it up. He had to get right down in the muddy water to push the tire on the wheel and fill the tire with air. It would soon be dark so he didn't dawdle. Finally the thing was fixed, turned around and started back down the hollow. About halfway back, it happened again! He just repeated the process and we hightailed it to the house.

After we got home and cleaned up (it's a wonder the shower drain and the clothes washer drain didn't clog!) Sue called. "What have you two been doing?"

"Oh, nothing much. We just took a leisurely walk. Your Dad needs to conserve his energy, you know."

– *CHAPTER 9* –

Flight—The Empty Nest

Good parents give their children roots and wings;
Roots to know where Home is
Wings to fly away and exercise what has been taught them.

We should have recognized the signs, but as parents we were quite new in the business of the romantic goings on that were affecting our children. Oh, they had their friends, all kinds, but marriage? Perhaps—somewhere in the distant future. But, yes, the clues were there: the Turner Creek egg truck came down Bowlings Creek frequently, and the driver was not delivering eggs; he was courting our daughter.

They spent lots of time together, on the porch swing, and at youth social activities and excursions. One sure sign was the shine in Rosie's eyes when Philip Swartzentruber's name was mentioned. Yet, I was emotionally unprepared for the inevitable.

"Could we talk with you two for a minute?" Philip seemed tense. He and Rosie were holding hands and approached her father and me in the kitchen.

"Sure." There was a question in Wesley's voice.

"Uh, Rosie and I want to get married and would like your permission and blessing." There was a long silence. Rosie looked scared.

"When?" I finally asked.

"Soon. This Winter, after Christmas." Another long pause. My emotions were kicking and screaming. *You are too young, Rosie, and this house absolutely won't be the same without you. Philip will be good for you . . . it's not that. I'll miss you!* I don't remember the rest of the conversation, but Wesley gave Rosie his permission and we assured them of our approval. Finally I went to bed but not to sleep.

"Why are your cheeks wet?" Wesley asked when he joined me.

"Have you ever heard of mommyitis? I haven't either, but I think I have it." Definition of the disease mommyitis: enlarging of the heart, a constriction in the throat, and water running from the eyes, accompanied by a combination of unexplainable feelings of sadness and joy and fear. The patient often has long periods of nostalgic remembering. . . .

I remember Rosie's long brown braids swinging as she and Ola Mae chased each other around the church yard; how she looked as she was kneeling on a rock in the middle of Bowlings Creek when her father/pastor poured water over her head for her baptizing. She was a devoted big sister to little sister Lisa. That tenderness was also evident in one episode Rosie told me about.

"We were riding home on the bus. I was in the third grade and Tommy and Gran were sitting behind me. Tommy had Gran's pocketknife and was teasing me, threatening to cut off my pigtail. I reached back to save my braid, and the knife cut a very small place in the palm of my hand. Grover stopped the bus, got out the first aid kit from under the seat, cleaned the cut, and applied some ointment. I guess he reported it to the principal, because the next morning Mr. Turner came into our room and gave Tommy a hard paddlin'. I felt so sorry for Tommy, 'cause I knew it was an accident and just a small cut."

Though Rosie was tenderhearted, she was not passive. She once preached a sermon to Gary Bellamy, on the bus. No known connection, but today Gary is a Spirit-filled Pentecostal preacher.

After Christmas, in 1977, there was a beautiful wedding at our little church. Wesley was rather nervous in his dual role of

New Moon Over Slick Rock Hollow

Father of the bride and officiating minister. Some invited guests decided not to come because of the dusting of snow. So, after the reception, we were left with a huge garbage can full of leftover punch! Give me a break—we had never been responsible for a wedding reception before. No problem with the punch, however. After the bride and groom left, our out-of-state overnight guests helped us eat Christmas cookies and drink punch and play rook half the night.

Leftover ham salad sandwiches was a more difficult matter. We finally stuffed them in the freezer and later sent them home with Rosie when they set up housekeeping at Buckhorn. "When you get married, you shake hands with cornbread and starvation." That's a country quote we sometimes hear when young people marry and leave home. For Philip it was ham salad sandwiches and starvation. He claimed when the bread got soggy, they threw the bread away and had bread-less sandwiches. He also accused me of sending soggy sandwiches along on their honeymoon!

Verda Rose, our little flower, was transplanted to bloom beyond the confines of Home. Today she is the mother of three and helps Phil pastor the Mennonite Church on Turners Creek.

* * * *

"Mom, you know that nice boy I told you about? He wants to come home with me next week, to spend the weekend. He wants to meet you all. Is that ok?" It was our daughter Fern, calling from her dorm at Berea College. There was excitement in her voice.

"You mean the one from Alabama?" My mind backtracked. I remembered the many times Gerald Metzler's name had come up and I was too naive to think this friendship was more then casual. "Bring him on. We don't have an extra bed, you know, but he can share the boys' room."

Bowlings Creek One-room School

That Friday evening when Gerald ducked his head to enter the kitchen I'm afraid I stared up into his face. *He is so tall! That quilt on Steve's bed will never cover all of him,* I thought. Gerald was soon a friend to the whole family. That visit was the first of many. Though I was not surprised when they came to us, hand in hand, announcing to us their intention of marriage, after graduation; still, I had a bad case of mommyitis.

Birmingham, Alabama is so far! I was secretly wishing Fern could be at home again for awhile after college. I know Gerald will be a super good husband; he is devoted to her and to the Lord. He will take good care of her. Still, a corner of my heart will go with my firstborn.

My mother died in 1957, so Fern doesn't remember her Grandmother Lapp. Yet I receive comfort in remembering that Mom and Dad came to visit from Pennsylvania, and that Mom hugged and loved Fern, her first grandchild from her marriage to my Dad. Fern was wearing her little pink coat and cap her other Grusmommy had made for her.

New Moon Over Slick Rock Hollow

It makes me smile to remember the squeals when Fern and Rosie slid down the bank outside our kitchen, on a makeshift sled, deep fluffy snow scattering everywhere. Fern's dark eyes sparkled and her black hair was covered with snow. Fern was a survivor. She had to be, the oldest in a family of nine children. I remember when her twin siblings were infants. I settled her and Rosie on the couch, a cushion under their left arm. Then I placed a crying baby in each lap and a warm bottle of milk in their right hand. The crying stopped and the big sisters smiled.

The first weeks of first grade at the one-room schoolhouse just down the creek were extremely difficult for Fern and her mother. When she left the house crying and came home sucking her thumb and crying, this mother cried too. But she survived with no permanent damage to her teeth or personality, and went on to Altro School, Breathitt High, Mount Carmel Mountain Holiness School, Rosedale Bible Institute, and Berea College.

Wesley and I both grew up speaking the Pennsylvania Dutch dialect of German before we spoke English. We wanted our children to learn that as well. Fern soon learned to speak the German Pennsylvania Dutch **and** the English Kentucky Mountain dialect. When she graduated from eighth grade at Altro School as valedictorian, she was required to give a speech. It was an excellent presentation but her father claimed her mountain accent was so pronounced, he could barely understand the speech!

Fern appeared serene in spite of the rapid changes in her life that June of 1979. She and Gerald graduated from Berea College, married several days later and moved to Birmingham. Me? I wasn't as calm. In those weeks before the wedding, I picked gallons of strawberries from my patch and squelched the panic. I made dozens of "to do" and "don't forget" lists—plans for shopping, meals, lodging for out-of-state guests, and how many gallons of punch *not* to make, and how to keep the punch from the color "yuck!" Oh, and make sure the boys put all the animals "up" so the goats don't amble into the church while the groom is saying "I do." Dear me, what will I wear? Never mind—the bride is center stage, not the mom.

Fern came home from Berea, hugged me and said, "Don't worry Mom. Everything will be fine." It was. Especially the flowers. Fern and her maid of honor, Laurie, climbed the hill behind the church and gathered wild flowers. They brought white daisies and yellow black-eyed Susans and pink phlox to the front porch and spent hours arranging them for the wedding.

The wedding and the day was beautiful in every way. I was sitting in the front pew of our church, by myself, since the bride's father was also the preacher doing the ceremony. I was thinking how sweet and beautiful the dark-eyed bride was, and how strong and steady the groom. Then—another attack of mommyitis. Not here! Not now! You will make a scene! Instead I mentally measured the punch—again. Then I prayed, "Jesus, tender Shepherd, hear me. Bless thy little lamb tonight. In the Unknown be thou near them; keep them safe in Eternal Light. They are leaving their parental fold, may they ever stay in your Heavenly fold."

Her name is Fern and she is thriving with quiet beauty as a true fern. She has used her varied and creative teaching skills in

Eighth grade graduation at Altro School, 1969.

New Moon Over Slick Rock Hollow 113

excellent ways in the country church at Straight Mountain just north of Birmingham, and on the job.

* * * *

"Steve Stoltzfus, do you take this woman by your side, Rebecca Fyffe, to be your wedded wife? Will you . . . " Wesley's voice was solemn, but in spite of the solemnity of the occasion, my mind began to wander.

Several years earlier, on a Saturday, Steve came to me as I was washing garden lettuce for Sunday's salad. "Mom, are the Fyffe's coming down for church tomorrow?"

"I think so and we'll eat lunch together. Polly is bringing some food. Why do you ask?"

"Oh, nothing, I just wondered. I wonder if Becky is coming."

For several years in the 1970's, Darrell Fyffe brought his family from Morgan County to our church nearly every Sunday. Steve's curiosity turned to friendship and eventually he fell in love with Becky, Darrell and Polly's beautiful blond daughter. He decided to marry her, but first he must finish high school, graduate from Rosedale Bible Institute, spend two years in the North Country of Red Lake, Ontario, as a missions volunteer and cycle with a friend to the West Coast and back. Becky waited.

Weddings do funny things to me. You know, mommyitis. Pictures danced through my memory. I saw Stevie on his sixth birthday. He was standing on the rock in the middle of Bowlings Creek early in the morning of July 16. He was still in his pajamas and clutching his security blanket. Me and Alex Williams, his little friend, were standing nearby watching the drama. Stevie had planned this event weeks in advance.

"I am six years old. I'm old enough to stop sucking my thumb. I don't need my blanket anymore. I'm going to throw my blanket in the creek!" With that, he flung his blanket into Bowlings Creek. It floated downstream, around the bend and out of sight, never to be seen again.

If anybody down river finds a yellow baby blanket snagged on a rock or branch, bring me a piece for a keepsake.

Another picture: The clan of children came storming into the kitchen. "Stevie is hurt! He fell off the bicycle and he's hurt." I found him out behind the church house beside his bike, holding his arm. His forearm was bent into a peculiar angle and I knew at once it was broken. Where it should have been straight, it was decidedly not.

"Ouch," was all he said.

"What happened?"

"Me and my buddies, the Turner boys, were riding round and round and round the church house real fast, some one way and some another, and I had a wreck." I nearly panicked. I knew this child must be taken to Home Place Hospital to have that bone set. I also knew I must take him because Wesley was gone to a church in Indiana for the week, and Frances wasn't here. *Will that old car get me there and is there even gasoline in it? Do I know the way for sure and will Stevie pass out on the way? It may be dark before we get back and who will stay with the other children? How will I pay for this? Lord! Help me!*

I calmed down and sent Roland Turner over to ask his Grandma if the others could stay with her for a while. I quickly rubbed my bare feet with a washcloth, found a pair of shoes and the car keys. Stevie climbed in the front seat beside me without a whimper and we were off. The Lord sat beside me also. Everyone was scurrying around and looking serious and I think Stevie rather enjoyed the attention.

Dr. Martin expertly set the bone and Wesley, when he returned, unbent the bicycle frame and untwisted the spokes on the wheel. Soon they were both in operation again and Stevie was back to riding his bike round and round with his friends.

I remembered another episode, several years and several bicycles later. Stevie never had much spending money so he had to take advantage of any financial opportunities that came along. One early spring day the mailman brought an opportunity for a business venture. A seed company sent Stevie a slick colorful brochure, with pictures of **huge** flower blossoms of all kinds, the reddest red beets and radishes, the largest yellowest pumpkins you never saw. Along with the attractive pictures was a proposition and a promise; you sell our seeds, we will send you money. If you sell enough, you will be eligible for all kinds of prizes: school supplies, perfume, toys, watches.

Several weeks later Stevie was outfitted with a box of ten-cent seed packets and an envelope for the money. His sisters had already gone door to door on Bowlings Creek, selling their seeds, so he set his sights higher—The Ridge of Gays Creek. He laced up his tennis shoes and set off on his old blue bicycle, the one without brakes and only one speed. It was hard pedaling to the head of Bowlings Creek and up the Gays Creek Hill, but he made it. Gardeners and housewives along the way felt sorry for him, I guess, and bought all his seeds. Now came the hard part, traveling **down** three miles of hills and curves on a bicycle with no brakes.

He came home exhilarated; he had sold his seeds! But I thought he seemed breathless and he had a funny limp in his walk. He took off his shoes and I saw a deep ridge worn in the rubber sole of his shoe—worn nearly through to the foot. "What's this?"

"Uh, well, you know my bike had no brakes (I didn't know), so I had to use my foot. I pressed my tennis shoe real hard against the tire, coming down the hills. It smoked some but it worked!" He was grinning. I don't remember what prize he got but I think he earned every prize in the book. His Dad had to buy him a new pair of tennis shoes.

"I do." Steve's strong affirmation brought me back to the church sanctuary in West Liberty. Like his Father, Steve always had a strong voice and a people pleasing personality. He hugged **all** the women at his wedding.

Though Becky and I are both in love with Steve, there is no rivalry. His Father and I have released him to follow his heart to make a home with Becky. They have a daughter, Sarah, and have been a vital part of the church and community of West Liberty, Kentucky.

* * * *

"So you are one of the twins." The visitor in our home was checking out Daniel as though he were an oddity or an interesting freak. Being a twin had those kinds of moments, but **having** a twin brother was definitely a plus. Someone to help with your projects and to share chores. No doubt about it, Daniel and David were best friends. Then Diane entered the picture.

"I thought you would wait until you are through college," I told Dan when he told us he and Diane Eash planned to marry.

"No way. We'll rent a little trailer off Morehead State University campus and we can be together."

"Of course." He and Diane were a good match and very much in love. Besides, Wesley and I both liked Diane also. Dan had made an excellent choice so why should we interfere?

The wedding, in June of 1982 was at the beautiful Log Cathedral in Buckhorn. The warm June breeze found the casement windows open, so it entered softly, fluttering the flower arrangements but was careful not to extinguish the white candles. I glanced above the podium at the oak Celtic cross that Wesley had made for the church, years ago. I was caught up in the beauty and solemnity of this celebration—the songs, the rose and white decorations, the flowers, but especially the beautiful bride and the handsome groom. Without warning, memories rushed into my thinking. Mommyitis.

Wesley's forebears, as far back as there are records, were farmers and/or craftsmen. The farmer gene bypassed Wesley but his son got a double portion. I remember the morning Daniel came to the house from doing before school chores. He was utterly devastated. His huge hog, the one he raised from a piglet and was now ready for market, the one who was expected to give a gain on Daniel's hard earned savings, was lying in the pen—dead. It apparently died of electrocution when it chewed into a live wire, overhead in the barn. *Why do these things happen when Dad is gone out of town for the week?*

"I'll have to bury it," is all he said when he left for school.

I remembered the array of creatures that paraded through our family years; some pets and some not, some confined and some running free, some outside and some—heaven forbid—inside! But nearly all were there because of Daniel and David. For those of you who are interested in the subject of goats, there is no fence high enough and no electric fence strong enough to keep them from consuming your most colorful flowers and your healthiest shrubs. There were dozens of chickens and pheasants and quail and half-breeds, all hatched in Wesley's handmade hatchery in the basement. There were several white Spitz dogs that had pups periodically. I remember when Daniel came up the road, crying and carrying a mangled Snowball. The dog had been hit by a car and was never the same again.

There were wild pets that were caged briefly and released: squirrels, chipmunks, raccoons, and opossum (very briefly). I walked into the living room one day and stopped. There was a peculiar smell. "Daniel!" I yelled. "Surely you didn't bring that skunk into the house, did you?"

"But Mom, he is de-scented and he would make a pretty house pet." Several months earlier Wesley and the boys found a family of motherless baby skunks. They sold them all but one to a pet shop. "Nappy," short for Napoleon was de-scented and brought home.

"He may be cute and he is de-scented, but he still stinks so out he goes," I told Dan. Nappy was banished to the barn. His latter years were spent mostly hibernated in a pile of straw.

Daniel's farm gene was most evident when he worked the soil. He dreamed of living and working on a "real" farm. All we could offer was 1/2 acre of hillside. So, Wesley rented a garden plot across the creek from the Cole clan. Later, when the boys were in college, we rented a large garden from Roscoe, several miles down the creek. The boys planted beans, potatoes, cabbage, and broccoli. Up close to the road they put a watermelon patch. From his porch Levi Combs watched with critical eye.

What do them boys know about gardening? Hit won't do no good there; the soil is too poor. Besides, if the melons do grow, somebody'll be sure to steal 'em. Those watermelon seeds sprouted, grew and produced some **huge** melons. Levi could tell they were heavy. He watched me check them out, pick one up and nearly topple over with the weight. I had to stop and rest several times before I got the brute melon to the car.

"Where did them boys larn to garden?" Levi asked Wesley.

"I reckon in agriculture classes at college. Their genes helped too."

I imagine Levi thinking. *You jest don't get that kind of larnin' from books! Or genes, whoever that is. But you cain't argue the evidence.*

Wesley's voice broke into my mind-rambling. "Dan, will you take this sister by your side. . . ." *Oh dear, I nearly missed the vows! I don't need to worry about the punch, but I hope Maxine made enough.*

"I do." Dan's strong voice.

"I do." Diane's soft but sure voice.

The Lord shook out Dan and Diane as salt in Mercer County, Kentucky, where they are settled with their four children. The farming lure is still very strong so he teaches other kids in the Vo. Ag.

program at Mercer County High School how to grow huge watermelon and hogs and how to make flower arrangements. The whole family is very involved with the people at a church in Danville.

* * * *

I watched the blue birds the day of their home-leaving. The first fledgling poked his head out the hole and looked around. Scared, he ducked back in. Again and again he repeated the exercise, each time leaning out a bit farther. The parent birds were fluttering about. "Just try it, come on out, you can fly!" Finally Junior took the plunge and made a successful flight to the nearby bush. Soon the second little one appeared and went through the same maneuvers. He had watched his sibling. "If he can do it, I can too." The third one didn't hesitate very long and soon joined the other courageous ones on the bush. The process of emptying the nest box was gaining momentum. The last two birds just went zip, zip, away.

Our Box is emptying just like those birds, I thought. *And they are leaving faster and faster!*

Iva Sue was a highly motivated child, anxious to get on with life, so immediately following her high school graduation, she confidently left the nest box and headed for Bible School, a job, college, Voluntary Service, and only God knows where else. I was left with much shorter apron strings. I wanted to stop up the door of our nest to keep the rest inside.

"He is just a friend, nothing more." Sue called us from Louisville, where she was doing volunteer church work. "His name is Bill Hooley and he is bringing me home next weekend on his motorcycle." Well! I soon saw through the facade of mere friendship. They were in love whether they knew it or not. A year or so later when Bill came to Wesley asking his permission to marry his daughter, we weren't too surprised. I thought, *What a fine son-in-law he will be. Strong and steady enough to calm Sue's fast drive.*

So we prepared for a June wedding, but we were totally unprepared for the next bit of drama.

Our seventh bird, Twila, had graduated from Breathitt High, attended Rosedale Bible Institute and was completing nurses training at Hazard Community College. She was also in love with a Jantzi boy from Michigan. One winter day Chuck Jantzi made an unexpected (to us, not to Twila) trip from Cedarville College in Ohio, to Kentucky to see Twila. He seemed rather nervous, partly because of his scary near-collision experience on the snowy Mountain Parkway, but mostly because he had something important on his mind.

That evening, Wesley and I were sitting at the kitchen table, reading. The other girls had gone to bed and we had left the two lovers alone in the living room. They strolled out to where we were and Chuck said, "Wesley, Twila and I plan to get married."

"Oh-yes-well-uh-that's nice-eventually. You still have several years of school ahead. . . ."

"No, I mean soon, in June. With your permission we want to have a double wedding with Bill and Sue." *Girls, you can't do this to me!* I did some serious grieving when the other girls left home, but surely I could keep Twila several more years. And it's not as though our daughters move next door or just down the road somewhere. No, they must move out of state and hundreds of miles away. And I never planned for our birds to fly two at a time!

Wesley was nearly speechless. He ran his fingers through his hair several times. Finally he said, "You can't be serious."

Gaining confidence, Chuck said, "I'm as serious as I can be." Twila just nodded her head. Her face was a picture of love and apprehension. This fine Jantzi boy who wanted to become our son-in-law was a purposeful young man; he knew pretty well which direction he was headed with his life. But he was not independent; he needed someone by his side. He chose Twila.

We discussed the situation. Wesley ran his fingers through his hair again. Finally we gave them our blessing. We have never regretted our permission for that decision.

The girls and I agreed to keep this wedding simple. However, there is nothing simple about a church wedding and reception for 300 guests. Ninety percent of those would also need lodging. The Jantzi's and the Hooley's and the Stoltzfus' all have many friends and family, near and far, who were honored to be included in the celebration.

"How much punch this time?" I asked Wesley. We decided on 20 gallons. Also 40 pounds of ham and 20 pounds of bologna, 30 dozen ice cream bars and 420 buns and . . . the list seemed endless.

Saturday, June 15, 1985. The organ loft at the Log Cathedral at Buckhorn was vibrating with joyous music from Uncle Dan Bowman. His eyes are blind but there is nothing wrong with his fingers on the organ keys. With the strains of "Here Comes the Bride," I stood with the congregation, turned, and saw a scene I will never forget.

The father of the brides, looking quite handsome and very proud, was strolling down the aisle with a beautiful bride on each arm. They were in perfect step and later I learned why. Even in a formal setting, it is very difficult for Wesley not to be casual. So, to keep everybody's jitters down, he was reciting under his breath, but loud enough for the girls to hear, "I-ne-ver-saw-a-purple-cow-I-ne-ver-hope-to-see-one-but-I-can-tell-you-now-I'd-rath-er-see-than-be-one."

With two brides and two grooms and two ceremonies and two cakes, the event was doubly beautiful. When the preacher-father said, "Ladies and gentlemen, may I present to you Mr. and Mrs. Hooley and Mr. and Mrs. Jantzi, I'm sure it was an emotional moment for Mother Hooley and Mother Jantzi. All I could think of was "will there be enough punch?"

It was the Monday after. The girls were on their Honeymoon, the guests all went home, and I crashed. Another case of mommyitis, and I began to reminisce.

Iva Sue had so many friends: Pam, Billie Jean, Donnie, America, Wanda, Susan, Marsha, to name a few. And especially Christine. She and Sue were church friends and stay-the-night friends. I can hear them singing on the church bus and in bed before sleep, "Which Road Leads to Heaven?" Iva Sue's eighth grade class had the distinction of being the last ones to graduate from Little Red School in 1975. After that the little red buildings situated on school campus in Jackson were demolished, except for one, which is a kind of museum.

"Mom, this skirt is too long! Can't we take it up an inch?" Those were the high school days of mini skirts and tanned legs. Iva Sue's father raved against sunbathing and I raved against short skirts. Somehow we all came through those years intact. The skirts went down and up and the sunbathing was done in seclusion, out of sight!

Back then, play was creative, not electronic or even mechanical. I remember the elaborate playhouse the girls created every summer, up on the hill under the old Oak. A garbage can lid was propped between tree branches for a stove, tin cans held up the wooden benches and shelves, and there was a fireplace made of stones and sticks.

Our children didn't have the opportunity to be involved in many after-school activities, like athletics or cheerleading. But they could pretend. There were many cheerleading routines performed on the church house steps. The girls' skirts got in the way so I suppose when I wasn't looking, they tucked them in their panties. As for joining the Girl Scouts, well—Sue recalls, "I remember the time Twila and I got our Girl Scouts honor from our big brother, Dan. The obstacle course was conducted on the Bowlings Creek. We had to walk on ice without breaking through, go through treacherous rapids, climb over rocks, and keep up with our fearless leader. Our reward was a four inch piece of yardstick with the date and accomplishment written on it."

Twila had friends also. I remember one in particular. Talk about imagination! I'll let Twila tell it. "My brothers would take me to my friend's house on their bicycle and later take me back home. We did anything from using suntan lotion for medicine, (yes, we actually made Carol eat the stuff!) to stealing green apples from Ervin Spicer's tree. My friend's daddy scolded us good for that. One day, we were playing in the shed and my friend took a bottle off the shelf and suggested we put some in our underwear. The bottle said "disinfectant," but if she thought the idea was fun, why not? So we did. As you know, disinfectant burns. We were on fire! We ran down to the creek and plopped down into the water for relief. I'm not sure of all the details after that, but I do remember I had a very uncomfortable ride home, sharing the banana seat of Steve's bike."

One day Twila came into her Daddy's shop crying hysterically. "What's the matter, child?" he asked.

"I-I-sob-didn't mean to-sob."

"Didn't mean to what?"

"I fed Daniel's Golden Pheasants and didn't shut the gate to the pen and they got out and flew away." More sobs.

"Come on, I'll help you catch them." They searched all over the hillside and found two under a rock. Later, after dark, with a flashlight, they spotted the rest roosting in a tree. All were rescued and Twila stopped crying.

When her big brothers went off to camp or youth retreat or to college, Twila was the one who cared for their critters and fowl and varmints and fish. Like the time the heating element in the tropical fish aquarium malfunctioned and the fish all fried! Twila gathered some icicles from the roof to cool down the temperature, but it was too late; the ice immediately melted and the fish were dead. She milked the goat and carried five gallons of water up the hill to the hog and turned the quail eggs in the incubator.

Today, Twila enjoys nursing and she enjoys even more caring for their four boys, in Ohio, Michigan, Pennsylvania, and wherever Chuck's job takes him. Sue and Bill are parents of three children. Sue also has a successful home business. All are involved in their local churches.

* * * *

Once a parent, always a parent. Your child sneaks his way into your heart and never leaves. Somewhere, along the way, he grows up and dries his wings and flies away. But the parent-child relationship continues across the years and miles.

It was early in January. Son Dave had confided to his brother that he was heading out to Phoenix, Arizona. "Or some place. I'll not go back to Morehead State but enroll at another university to get my teaching degree."

"By yourself?"

"Yeah. Well, why not? I'll take in some sights on the way, maybe go around by Texas, and who knows where else; just follow my inclinations. Mom and Dad both have some relatives in Phoenix, I think. I'll look them up when I get there."

So he set out in his car with a sleeping bag and little else.

These parents began to worry. Then I thought about the alternate route to worry—trusting prayer. "Lord, I know this boy of ours is a grown man, capable of making decisions and taking care of himself. I am no more responsible for all that. But, Lord, he seems rather lonely and unsettled. Just keep watch over him, and if there is a good wife for him somewhere, help him find her."

We heard snatches of his where-abouts and what-abouts. He traveled through the southwest, sleeping in his car, inquiring at some universities in Texas, experiencing a little of the seamy side of

New Moon Over Slick Rock Hollow

Mexico, and praying for a wife. On to Phoenix. In June he drove 2000 miles home to the double wedding of his two sisters, still lonely. This time he took his dog, Dottie Lou, back with him. Now he had someone to talk to and to share his doughnuts with. Again we heard snatches. He stayed in one of Skip's rented trailers awhile; worked part time with a construction crew; found some friends in a church; moved into a cheap apartment with no refrigeration, so on the few occasions when Dave splurged on ice cream, he and Dottie Lou had to eat the half-gallon at one sitting; enjoyed the Arizona climate. Tuition at the University of Arizona took most of his wages, so he ate a lot of Sapps day-old doughnuts and generic macaroni and cheese, with an occasional hamburger he shared with Dottie Lou!

One day I had a call from Rosie. "Mom, Dave called and guess what? He has a girlfriend! He seems to have fallen in love, hard. She is Lois Crossgrove from Ohio and won't be in Phoenix very long so he says he 'has to make hay while the sun shines.'" Apparently the sun kept shining and Dave kept on making hay. Dottie Lou had to move over.

The wedding was at Lois' home church at Lockport, Ohio, in December of 1987. It was simple and beautiful and positively joyous. "Thank you Lord," I prayed. "The groom is no longer lonely." When the officiating minister (also the groom's father) searched for my eyes and winked, I knew he too was having an emotional moment. Without warning, I felt the symptoms of mommyitis.

Sometimes I referred to our three sons as the triplets; they were nearly one size. Dave and Dan shared the same birthday and Steve was only 17 months older. However, we soon learned they had very distinct personalities and abilities. Dave's ability to create things with his hands stemmed from a long line of craftsmen. So one summer when the twins and the two Willett boys built their log cabin, it was not only a boyhood fun project; it was also an outlet for their creative energies. I wasn't there so I don't know who was the architect and who was the boss or who was the builder, but I would guess

David did the more intricate parts like placing the logs just right, then chinking between the logs and smoothing the dirt floor.

The hut was situated on a slightly level spot up the hollow across from our house. It was an "x," with a loft, a door and a tin roof. First they felled the trees; one hatchet for four boys, which was a good thing. That way the blisters on their hands could take a break. Bill Willett helped out. He hitched his little pony to a piece of tin and she dragged it up the hill to the building site. He also found an old stove somewhere but the boys could never get it to draw very well. Dave remembers finding a spot of clay on the creek bank. He dug some out and carried it up the hill in a five gallon bucket to chink the logs.

Later, when the twins were in college, they helped their father build some nice houses and bridges, but none were as fine as that little log cabin up the narrow hollow on Bowlings Creek.

Sometimes a boy and a dog will share a special comradeship. For David, there was Scotty, a nondescript, shaggy, part Collie mongrel, with lots of battle scars. Later there was Dottie Lou. He taught her about obedience and she taught him about devotion. Sometimes, in Dave's roaming here and there, Dottie had to stay at home with us. She took advantage of her freedom and began roaming the hills.

"Have you seen Dottie Lou? She hasn't been here to eat for two days." Lisa was worried. We called and looked and waited, afraid to tell Dave she was missing. One quiet morning a week or two later, I was hanging our clothes and I heard a faint whimper away up on the hill, across the creek behind an old barn. Lisa and her daddy climbed the hill, following the cry. They found Dottie Lou, with her front paw caught in a steel trap. She was very glad to see them and promised to stay closer to home!

I remember when 120 Bible School students were crammed into our small church building. With a dozen separate classes, it's impossible to keep the noise level below "loud." Teacher voices are not confined to a 12x12 curtained cubicle. Through the curtain I

New Moon Over Slick Rock Hollow 127

heard Dave's teaching voice and I thought, *He is an excellent teacher. He teaches with authority and compassion. The kids love him. Perhaps he will make teaching his career.*

Today Dave and Lois live in Archbold, Ohio, and are the parents of five boys, including a set of twins. Dave teaches at a public school and gives leadership to their local House Church. He also crafts intricate knives and furniture pieces, and he still raises chickens and birds and Dottie Lous.

* * * *

Our baby bird is gone. She had been peeking out the door of our nest, watching the others fly away, feeling a little restless and alone. Finally she took short practice flights to Rosedale, Ohio; to Dayton, Ohio; to Martha's Vineyard in Massachusetts; and to Cedarville College. Then she packed her bags for a permanent leaving. But not alone. Keith Miller had persuaded Lisa to fly away with him.

For Wesley and me it doesn't get any easier to watch our young'uns leave home. And this was our baby.

Another wedding. Another beautiful bride on her father's arm. Another June celebration at the Log Cathedral. This was daughter number six and child number 8. The father of this clan had the privilege of asking those solemn, commitment-filled questions of all 18: "Will you take this woman (man) by your side? Will you love and cherish her (him) until death do you part?"

There was always a confident "I will. I do." Great.

Those questions weren't hard for the bride and groom. For Mom and Dad, the emotion-filled question, the question that flipped your heart and filled your eyes and closed your throat, wasn't that easy. "Who gives this bride away?" *Will you give this bride away? Do you promise to release her to the Lord and to her husband?* **Will you let her go?**

"I do."

At the May wedding in 1994 I tried to keep my skittering thoughts on neutral things, on non-emotional things. Like, *will there be enough punch for the reception? Oh dear, Twila's boys are getting really restless.* Things like that. But suddenly I had no control; my thoughts insisted on scurrying back to Lisa's growing-up years. Mommyitis.

Ten-year-old Lisa was sitting in her new bean bag chair, holding Punkin. It was Christmas Day and she was introducing her cat to her bird. "Listen, Punkin, this is Pretty Bird. I just got her for Christmas, so she will live here too. You must not bother her." Punkin and Lisa understood each other and the cat never bothered the parakeet.

Punkin was a Siamese, very independent, smart and feisty; also loyal and jealous. Lisa eventually went off to college and only came home occasionally. Punkin stayed at home. She seemed to sense when Lisa would be coming home; she perched outside Lisa's bedroom window and howled. Honest. But one weekend Lisa brought along her friend, Michelle. Here was a threat to the girl-cat friendship. You have to understand that Punkin was house broken and that she never got on any furniture. That Sunday morning we all, except Punkin, went to church. Michelle left her large cloth bag, full of books and papers and personal things, lying on the couch in the living room. When we got home, that cat had urinated **all over** Michelle's bag, just for spite.

I remember Lisa's high school days. She and I took those early morning walks to the bus stop, after we moved to Slick Rock Hollow. When it was muddy she carried her clean shoes and I carried back home her muddy shoes. By afternoon the mud was settled and she walked on home. I remember several days before her high school graduation that her friend drowned in a swimming accident. Lisa came home from school, very distraught. "Jody drowned!" She choked on each word. She took the phone into the bathroom and called her friend Angie. She and Angie talked and cried for an hour.

New Moon Over Slick Rock Hollow

That was a very difficult funeral and graduation for Breathitt High School.

Abruptly my thoughts slid back to the cathedral and to the celebration at hand. "May I introduce to you Mr. and Mrs. Keith Miller!" I thought I heard a tremor in Wesley's voice. Through applause and tears, Keith's mother and I exchanged a look, *I know what you are feeling.*

Then our baby bird was gone. Like her siblings, she comes back, back to the home nest and back to the hills. "It's so flat in Ohio, and Columbus is so city." Followers of Jesus are salt and light. I'm sure Columbus could use both of those commodities.

Recently Lisa called. "Dad, Mom. Keith and I are coming next weekend. Could we bring Thor along?"

"Who?"

"Thor."

"Thor who?"

"He is our new black Labrador dog. He is pretty big." (That was an understatement. He looked like a huge bear!)

Wesley hesitated. He had a childhood flashback: a neighbor's Lab had clamped its teeth into Wesley's leg, pulled him off his bicycle and laid him up with blood poisoning for six weeks.
"Oh, but Thor is friendly, very docile," Lisa assured us.

So now it's Thor instead of Punkin. I'm thinking Lisa will always have a special pet. Besides that, she now has two little ones to care for—children, not pets.

* * * *

I tried to calm her down, but Carol was on cloud nine and wouldn't come down. "Mom! Guess what! Jim has asked me for a date! He is at home now and he called me at Bethel Camp and we're going. . . . " On and on she went. Her excitement fairly rattled the telephone. Finally I yelled, "Wait!" through her flustered chatter.

"Jim who?"

"You know, James Monroe Riley from Gays Creek. I call him Jim and we are getting acquainted and he asked me for a date and . . . !"

Of course, I thought, but James has been single nearly 40 years and has been a bachelor on his own for a number of years. He has been in the Navy and has seen the world. And Carol has been on a short-term mission trip and has worked and lived in Ohio. They have both been single long enough to become independent. What makes them think anything will change now?

But things did change, dramatically. Jim and Carol fell deeply in love and planned for marriage, but not until Jim received his nursing degree. By then, Wesley was ready to give them his blessing when James asked permission to marry his daughter. By then, I was ready to receive, without reservation, this Riley boy into our family clan.

With James' dramatic flair and Carol's excitability, the wedding was decidedly different and uniquely theirs. The Buckhorn Log Cathedral was James' growing-up Presbyterian Church so it was natural to have the wedding there in June, 1997. Back when Mr. Mattoch built those buildings, there was no thought of air conditioning. It was a hot humid day in late June and I was afraid Carol would pass out under all those yards and yards of heavy satin and lace. She didn't.

The music was a concert. The pipe organ was grand, the bride sang the "Lord's Prayer," accompanied on the piano by her groom. The Stoltzfus nieces and nephews nearly stole the show with their rendition of "Shine, Jesus, Shine!" James regaled the guests with his stories of his and Carol's romance, of how the Lord brought them together. Once again Wesley walked down the isle with a beautiful bride on his arm, only to give her away.

"Here Comes the Bride." Without warning, Mommyitis hit, hard. In my mind I was back at our "growing-up" house, watching Carol grow up.

I remember her sitting on the homemade couch, the one beside the shelf with the small table radio. She was listening to WMTC Radio, for two reasons. She was enjoying one of her favorite programs: Lum and Abner or Uncle Charlie and Aunt B. or Stories of Great Christians. And she was waiting to hear, "There will be no school in Breathitt County tomorrow." In the winter of 1977 and 1978, Breathitt County schools had a six-week vacation due to the weather. From Christmas vacation until March 1 it snowed and sleeted and froze every few days, just enough to keep the school buses off the dangerous hills and icy hollows. It was frustrating. Some call it family togetherness; others call it cabin fever or frenzied motherhood. It was all of that. The twins and Sue and Twila honed their table tennis techniques in the basement that winter. Carol sat by the radio to crochet or to embroider.

During those years at home she crocheted all kinds of afghans and doilies and ornaments.

For a school assignment, Carol wrote this:

> *One Sunday morning I was feeling really mean. I acted terrible in Children's Church. After Church the lady in charge of Children's Church told my Dad. "Carol hasn't been a nice girl today. I tried to send her upstairs to sit with her Mother, but she refused." I ran to the house, went into a back bedroom and cried, waiting for Dad. When he came, he talked to me a long time about what I had done and why he was punishing me. Then he spanked me. After that he took me into his arms and gave me a big hug. Then he prayed for me.*

One November, Carol hinted to her Daddy, "All I want for Christmas is a guitar." Music was in her genes, so her Dad hunted around and found an old guitar for her. After that she spent hours in her room with the guitar and a thick notebook of handwritten songs. I lay in bed and listened to her singing. She didn't know I was worshipping with her.

Carol remembers the feeling of joy when she and Cheryl Eash kneeled on the rock in Bowlings Creek to be baptized. I remember the feeling of deep thankfulness. So thankful that all of our children received the Lord's salvation and were baptized. I was so thankful also, that their father could do the baptizing for all of them.

"Carol, will you take this man by your side as your husband? Will you . . ." I'm back at the Log Church, wondering, it's *so hot and there are so many guests. Will there be enough punch?*

After serving a year in Chile on a mission's assignment, Jim and Carol are back in Lexington. Jim serves the Lord by preaching at times and by helping trauma patients in a hospital emergency room. Carol is happy with her sewing machine, her crochet hook, and her music. They are the adoptive parents of Sarah Elizabeth Ann, born in China.

* * * *

So I clean house. Armed with plastic bags and a resolute mind, I gather up years of accumulated "useless" paraphernalia: remnants of wedding napkins; test papers from B.H.S.; a tanned goat hide; a long peach-colored bridesmaid dress with long gathered sleeves; books—anything from chewed up nursery rhymes to college textbooks with carefully underlined pertinent truths; jigsaw puzzles with missing pieces; a teddy bear with a missing ear; small, beribboned and besmeared crafts from countless V.B.S. and Camp projects. (Bless those teachers for their infinite patience!)

I should be ruthless. I should be listening to my practical mind. Instead, my sentimental heart takes over. I find I am reverently touching each meaningless useless treasure and placing them back in the drawers and boxes. The Salvation Army will have to wait.

* * * *

He looked at his wife of forty years.
"Are the children gone?"
"Yes."
"All of them?"
"Yes."
"But they'll come back to visit."
"Of course."
"And there's always the grandchildren."
"Oh yes."
"Thank God for our family."
"Amen."
"Come. I want to hold you. I still have you. You still have me."
"I'm coming."

– CHAPTER 10 –

Bowlings Creek Mennonite Church

Bowlings Creek Reflections
by Wesley Stoltzfus

On the last Sunday of 1998 I handed my "mantle" to Calvin Eash. It was an emotional moment when I literally removed the coat from my back—the coat I "always wore," my wife said, and gave it to Calvin, along with some tools for the trade: a clean handkerchief in one pocket symbolized helping the hurting, the crying and the repentant; a capsule of smelling salts in the other pocket was for the distraught at funerals. That little ceremony emphasized my termination as Pastor of the Bowlings Creek Mennonite Church. Is this the end of my ministry in Eastern Kentucky? The question can't be ignored, and it was partially answered when Goldie Combs died a few days later.

"Wesley, could we bring Pappy to your church on Bowlings Creek for the funeral? And would you and Johnny Herald preach his funeral?" Yes, they could and so it was arranged. So, as the Lord gives me strength and unless He leads otherwise, I will continue to serve my Father in Heaven and my people in Kentucky.

The ministry continues. How did it begin? I was raised in a Beachy Amish home and church in Lancaster County, Pennsylvania. My family and my church family were godly people, but at that time there was little emphasis on helping people outside our circle, or for evangelism. There were, however, some seeds for evangelism planted in my young heart. I vividly recall one day when a young man, Carpenter by name, was at my father's farm doing electrical work. He told my father, "I'm leaving my job and Lancaster County. I'm moving my family to Atmore, Alabama to be a missionary and to start a church." I was impressed. John Groff was another seed dropper. He was a preacher in the Mennonite Church and was also my Dad's feed supply man. After he delivered our feed he would sit on a sack of feed for a few minutes to talk with me personally; to encourage me spiritually and to tell me about the new mission churches the Lancaster Conference was planting in South Alabama.

Soon after I had a conversion experience at age 19, I began to sense that the Lord wanted me to preach. I don't know how I knew; I just knew. That sense became very strong and I was willing, yet somewhat confused. The "when" and the "where" were not at all clear. The Lord didn't say, "You will preach for nearly 50 years in the hills of Kentucky." Rather, the plan unfolded, one page at a time. Along with the call to preach came the sense that I must give a year of my life to the Lord in some type of volunteer work. I don't know how I knew; I just knew. Our church had no VS opportunities so I volunteered to the mission outreach of the Conservative Conference. Leroy Slabaugh, Ivan Troyer and I were sent to Frank Dutchers on Bowlings Creek for two weeks, to build a fence. The other boys moved on; I stayed for nine months. Those few months were long enough for the Lord to develop within me a love for the mountain people and a vision for service and evangelism. I also began to develop preaching and teaching skills.

Then I was drafted for military service. The U.S. government provided an opportunity to alternate service for those of us who are opposed to military action. We were called Conscientious Objectors and were assigned to serve in designated hospitals or other state institutions. I had promised the Lord a year in volunteer work. When I was drafted, that promised year wasn't over. So I combined my obligation to the government with my self-imposed obligation to the church. I volunteered two years to Mennonite Central Committee and was sent to Mississippi State Hospital in Jackson, Mississippi, which was also government approved for alternate service to the military.

Those next two years were not lost to the Master's plan. Working in a state institution gave me lots of practice in practical ways of service. Caring for bed-ridden old men with deranged minds and young men with twisted emotions left little room for a grandiose dream of being a sainted missionary.

This was the segregated Deep South, with well-defined rules for relating to the "other" race. I broke the rules. Periodically, I ventured by myself across the river to the "Gold Coast," a small section of the city, rife with crime and poverty and especially bootleggers. Equipped with a stack of evangelistic church papers called "The Way," I walked the streets, offering a paper at every house and bar. Few refused.

During my second year in Mississippi, Martha and I were married. We had no idea where to go or what to do after my term expired. I was afraid to go back to Lancaster County; afraid I would be buried in a materialistic system and lose my vision. **And** I hated to milk cows! We didn't hesitate long when Frank Dutcher wrote and asked us to move to Bowlings Creek and for me to work at the saw mill. We moved into a little red house on the banks of Bowlings Creek in the spring of 1955. We immediately became involved in the life of the church and community—preaching, teaching, visiting.

When the Dutchers left just before the Big Flood in January 1957, it seemed appropriate for me to pick up Frank's mantle. Then we got a letter from our conference mission board. "Wesley, would you stay on in Frank's place until we find another preacher?" Forty-two years later, another one was found—Calvin Eash. In the meantime we stayed on and I was ordained in 1958 and we began serving under the leadership of Rosedale Mennonite Missions.

Mission Board members have come and gone, but I can honestly say we had a good working relationship with each group. Our whole family scurried about when we knew the Field Director was coming to visit. The kids put on their best behavior and tried to decide which one would give up his bed for the visitor. Martha cleaned the bathroom and mixed up a batch of fresh bread. I quickly tried to formulate some goals for the coming year, and reviewed our financial status, ready to lay everything out on the table.

Our conference churches sponsored us financially, with half support, for nearly forty years. The other half came from my work. While we were raising our family that work was sparse, and many times we didn't know how we would pay our bills and our taxes, or how to buy shoes for the children, and how to keep our vehicles running on the muddy rutted roads. However, neither the Lord nor the Mission Board had promised us an easy road. Back then, the Women's Service Committee was a tremendous help, especially for Martha. Every year somebody brought boxes and boxes of canned and frozen food. Unpacking those boxes was almost like Christmas!

In the 1960s, Mark Peachy was secretary of the Mission Board. He lived in Plain City, Ohio, and had the office in his home. Several times a year I took a small truck load of coal to Plain City to sell. Then I backed up to Noah Beachy's barn and loaded my truck with hay for our cow. While in Plain City I always stopped to see Mark. He became my mentor and helped me sort through problems and emotions in regard to my preaching and my vision. I was free to be open and honest with him and he listened.

Many times I felt totally inadequate for the task of being a missionary preacher. I had no formal training whatever beyond the eighth grade at Snake Hill One-room School. There was no orientation and no questionnaires. The Word says, "And ye need not that any man teach you, but as the Anointing teacheth you of all things . . ." For me, this is a literal truth. Starting when I was a young man at home, I began reading and studying the Bible, taking notes and journaling. Studying and preaching was and continues to be, a difficult discipline, but also a joy. I was influenced in my preaching by great preachers like Alvin Swartz and Aquilla Stoltzfus. They exemplified compassion and zeal. My Kentucky preacher brothers taught me to preach **only** the Bible—King James word for word preaching. I learned from them to keep personal illustrations and stories at a minimum. After all, Biblical illustrations are much more powerful.

In the early days of the Mennonite Churches in Eastern Kentucky (1950s and 1960s), Allegheny, Virginia, Ohio, Indiana-Michigan and Conservative conferences all had mission churches in Eastern Kentucky. Every summer we all came together for a week of fellowship and preaching and singing. Most of the churches were somewhat isolated, so we really needed each other. Each February I traveled with other brothers to Ministers Fellowship and every August we loaded up the family and went to Conference. Those were tremendous times of encouragement and learning.

Next to preaching, I suppose the most fruitful and fulfilling part of my ministry was what I call community pastoring. There were countless hours of sitting with the sick and dying. There were hundreds of funerals where I was privileged to minister to many, many people. There were pregnant mothers who needed a ride to the doctor or midwife, fast. There were miles of travel, taking people to Jackson for commodities, to Hazard for a doctor, to Lexington for a hospital, up a rough hollow to see a sick relative, and many places in between. Many times we heard, "Wesley, can you come? We need help." How could I refuse? There were scores of broken down or stuck-in-the-mud vehicles. Also, radios and furnaces and quilt frames and roads and bridges that needed repairs.

It seems to me the Holy Spirit equips each congregation for one facet of ministry; a strong focus in "doing" church. The focus for the Bowlings Creek Church has been teaching. We have been blessed with many excellent teachers, some who have been teaching

Sunday School, Vacation Bible School, camp and women's groups faithfully and effectively for many years. Though our area is very rural and sparsely populated, hundreds of children and youth have been taught in Sunday School and Vacation Bible School. For many years, our little congregation sponsored annually a two week V.B.S. at Gays Creek, at Bowlings Creek, at Keneva Hollow, and at Otter Creek. Some of those youth became Christians and have been actively involved in other churches, other denominations, other places. I don't regret this. In fact, that is one of my greatest sources of encouragement. If we have been privileged to help salt the earth for the Master, we are grateful.

For several years we had 130 in V.B.S. attendance. Thirty or forty were hauled in from Gays Creek. Because of our limited facilities and because of rivalry between Breathitt County and Perry County, we sometimes had minor feuds and riots! But some of the Gays Creek kids made decisions for Christ and after that we had special weekly youth meetings in their community.

Our congregation didn't do those Bible Schools alone. Each summer the Conference Mission Board sent dozens of young people into Eastern Kentucky as volunteer Bible School teachers. We hosted perhaps a dozen volunteers for several weeks in our home each year. That certainly wasn't always easy for the family, but saw it as another vital area of ministry. We needed the teachers and those young people needed the exposure to missions and to another culture. We still have friendship ties with many of those volunteers. More recently, as our conference youth found it more difficult to leave their jobs and their cars for several weeks of V.S. and as we became more autonomous, we have been able to staff our Bible Schools with our own people.

If our congregational strength is teaching, what are our weaknesses? I'm afraid we are content in our own little group with our own agenda, and have at times lost our zeal for bringing people to Jesus. Many of us, when we try to assess a pastor's ministry, think in terms of preaching, teaching, serving the community, and building a congregation. Too often we exclude the pastor's family as one of his projects. When our children were small a friend voiced her concern. "Surely you won't be raising your family in Kentucky, will you?" I figured since the Lord wanted my wife and I in Kentucky, He certainly wanted our children here also. We have never regretted that decision. My family needed a pastor-father as desperately as anybody. To be honest, though, it has been a constant struggle to know who needs my first attention in some situations. When the funeral of a brother in the church happens on the same day as your daughter's very important piano recital, what do you do?

Our children were a great asset in my ministry. They were salt and light in the public schools, among their friends and peers. Sometimes they were ridiculed for their high morals, but usually they were respected. Even today, when we meet Mr. Sebastian, a former Breathitt County school superintendent, he always asks about our family, where they are and what they are doing. Invariably he speaks words of praise about them. Our children also helped in the life of the church. Sadly, because of the stressed economy in Eastern Kentucky, scores of young people every year must leave home for work. They migrate to Ohio, Indiana, and Michigan. Our children were no exception. Now they are salt and light in other places and in other churches.

Certainly the children's mother was a big factor in every area of my life and ministry. Although Martha didn't have the same sense of "call" I did, she shared my visions from day one. She has always been my most ardent fan and encouraged me in every way. She said to me, "You are mine, but I do not own you exclusively."

After almost 50 years of living and working in Eastern Kentucky, there is much joy in reflecting. There are also some regrets. I regret that we didn't have a bigger harvest in the second and third generations of our people. Yes, I have failed in many ways. Yet I dare not focus on my regrets and failures. Rather, I must take

New Moon Over Slick Rock Hollow 141

them all to the cross of Jesus. My God has a 100% success record of redeeming mistakes and regrets and impossible situations. My faith rests in that truth.

Introducing Our Church
(For *The Brotherhood Beacon,* October 2002)

A dozen or more children were lined up at the front of the church. It was the end of a Sunday School quarter, and interest was high. Who would get a silver dollar coin? Lloyd began to call names while P. R. reached deep into his pocket and handed a special reward to each child with perfect Sunday School attendance for the past four months. There was much excitement and applauding and praising the Lord. A year earlier we had hit a dry spell—too few children at church. Our church is traditionally a "Sunday School" church so we became concerned. We prayed, "Lord, if you will send us more children, we will love them." He did and we are. We prayed and cried and hit the by-ways. Some fed hot dogs to the kids, some provided transportation and some helped create a hunger for God. Once again the children came.

Our church is located in the heart of Kentucky Appalachia, a very rural location, hard between a creek and a hill. It's a constant challenge to have sufficient parking space. The church was built and established in 1948 under the direction of the Mission Board of the Conservative Conference. Frank Dutcher was the first missionary-pastor, followed by Wesley Stoltzfus. Calvin Eash is the present pastor.

We love the Lord and love our little church. We get all excited about answers to prayer and how the Lord is at work among us. We even get excited when the numbers on the attendance roster reach over fifty! We have several preachers and teachers in training in our congregation, also home-school moms and foster moms and stay-at-home moms.

You ask, "What is your worship style?" It's a little hard to describe: a nice mix of traditional hymns, Fanny Crosby-style Gospel songs, Southern gospel, children's choruses, mountain and four part harmony, all without accompaniment.

Our services are rather informal—much visiting before and after. (We love to be together!) Preaching has high priority. It's solid, Bible based, convicting, convincing, and inspiring. Our pastor, Brother Eash, has been well trained, sitting in the classrooms of R.B.I.'s best. More than that, he habitually kneels under the training of the Holy Spirit. He and his wife Mary are a great team. He preaches and teaches, she plans the practical things.

They don't do it alone, however. We all help. We have to. Someone needs to teach all those kids at Sunday School and V.B.S. and children's church (60% of our assembly on Sunday morning is children). Someone needs to help at Bethel Camp, clean the church windows, and build a handicap ramp. The sick need a visit and the bereaved need a hug. The bills must be paid and the curriculum ordered. Women's and youth activities need a leader. So we all get on our knees and roll up our sleeves, alternately, and "do" church.

Though we are a small church in a remote hollow, we count it a holy privilege to be part of a huge congregation, the Church of Jesus Christ.

Mama and the Preacher

I married Wesley when we were young and I soon became a preacher's wife. At Wesley's ordination, he was given some responsibilities and guidelines for preaching and teaching and pastoring and evangelizing. Everyone understood what he was expected to do—visit the sick, bury the dead, encourage the saints, condemn sin and love the sinner, help the poor, and preach Christ. The whole bit. But what was **I** supposed to do? Nobody told me, but I found out—teach Sunday School and Vacation Bible School

New Moon Over Slick Rock Hollow 143

Vacation Bible School at the Gays Creek Campgrounds, sponsored by Ruth Yoder in the 1970s.

for 40 years, lead women's activities, raise the preacher's children, "look good around the palace," entertain expected and unexpected guests, and horror of horrors—speak in public and even at conference!

Let me tell you, I was totally and absolutely unprepared and incapable and inept. Let me tell you also wherever God puts you He trains you! God uses wherever you are to grow you. I claim 1 John 2:27. Don't worry if you don't have formal training, the Holy Spirit teaches you about all things.

Of course we have to be teachable. The pot can't say to the potter, "Why are you making me like this?" The quilt can't say to the quilter, "Why are you doing me this way? I would rather be another design and another color." But the quilter and the potter constantly keep in mind an image of the beautiful finished product. However, you and I are not inanimate quilts or pots. We are people, capable of saying "No" to our Creator. That's disastrous. Don't do that. Embrace life the way our God gives it and be molded and beautified in this process called life.

Our children grew up as preacher's kids, which was no big deal. To them the preacher was just Dad. And there were definite advantages. They learned early on how to "do" church; how to sweep the tile church floor and how to polish the second-hand pews. You do it this way: spray on Pledge and then scoot up and down the pews on your sitter. Then come Sunday, you watch with amusement as Granny Lizy sits down hard and nearly slides down to the floor! They learned to sing and to behave in Sunday School, sometimes.

They practiced their teaching and preaching at their father's suggestions. They learned how to organize a fellowship meal and how to care for the hurting. They learned that preachers are real people and what a blessing to have the visiting evangelist in our home, even though they had to give up their bedroom. They learned hospitality and discipline. I suppose there were disadvantages to raising a family in the parsonage but I can't think of any.

Our house sometimes looked and sounded like a tornado in a zoo. You know, eerie brain-splitting noise and knee-deep clutter. So what does this little woman do? This woman who functions best in calm and quiet order? Well, the Potter did some brain changing, so I learned to tolerate the chaos and even enjoy it! And my children rise up and call me "Blessed."

I was glad when they said unto me, "Let us go into the house of the Lord." Glad? Hardly. A houseful of noisy kids to get ready for church, keep the house quiet so the preacher can finish out his sermon (invariably someone was grouchy or sleepy or hungry), clear the kitchen table for a Sunday School class, be ready to teach a class of unrullies at Sunday School. (I had fallen asleep preparing my lesson the night before.) And what in the world shall I fix for lunch? There is no McDonalds within 50 miles. I'm sure the sermon was great but I don't know.

New Moon Over Slick Rock Hollow 145

In retrospect, what do I see? Well, we formed good habits. We said, "This is Sunday morning and we go to church, no questions." And in spite of distractions at church, God had a chance to get to me, and He did. In those times, I often heard the voice of God, sometimes unexpectedly. Yes, I often fell asleep preparing for a class, but those study times were the times I learned my Bible. One of the best ways to get good Bible training is to teach a Sunday School class or a Bible class of some kind. My pupils may not have learned much, but I did.

As you may guess, one of the challenges of being the wife of Wesley and the mother of his children was his pastor's heart. Why was that a problem? Well, he loves to minister and care for people. He gets a rush from conducting a funeral because the people appreciate his encouragement so much, and tell him so. Then he comes home to another kind of congregation—quarrelsome, grouchy, ungrateful children, and a tired-to-the-bone wife. It's much easier to comfort a grieving mother at the funeral. So Wesley had this constant conflict—*who comes first? Church or family?* Don't hear me wrong, he did an excellent job of juggling the two, but it wasn't easy. And it wasn't easy for me to deal with.

Wesley and I were both raised in a Beachy Amish community. Then we moved into an Appalachia Hill community. It was like transplanting into a foreign country. And, we thought we could teach them a few things. We thought the Lancaster County Mennonite workaholic culture was much better than the casual unhurried lifestyle of Kentucky and Tennessee and West Virginia. We interpreted their culture as lazy. We didn't think they raised their children right, and their housekeeping was so primitive and sloppy, I thought. And, of course, their accent was hard to understand. The Lord had to deal with us, big time, exposing our pride, arrogance and hatred, as sin. We began to be broken and our judgmental attitude turned to fascination.

We thought it was so interesting to live among the people of "There's a little pine log cabin, waiting down in Welcome Valley."

146   *New Moon Over Slick Rock Hollow*

Christmas service at Bowlings Creek Church, December 1962.

All the books and movies about the mountain folk were fascinating. And the hills are beautiful in spring.

The Lord continued to break us. We needed to move deeper in our relationship with the people, deeper than fascination. Gradually we learned to respect and love the people, and to accept them just the way they are. They are absolutely a special breed of people.

Finally, we are one of them. It was a long process and continues. There is a mutual respect and acceptance and love. However, we will always retain our first culture. We can't and don't want to deny our Amish Mennonite Pennsylvania roots. But it is possible to be bi-cultural.

We faced another difficult challenge through the years. The problem of poverty is complex and there are no easy answers. The longer we deal with it the fewer answers we have. I'm sure, like Jesus said, there will always be the poor. Perhaps the problem is with the rich rather than with the poor. Jesus looked at Mary who was pouring out (wasting) her past year's wages on his feet instead

New Moon Over Slick Rock Hollow 147

Christmas service at Bowlings Creek Church, December 2001.

of giving it to the poor. Jesus said to Judas, "You will always have the poor with you." In light of that, we need to pour out our riches at the feet of Jesus, in love and devotion. And, like Mary, listen to His words.

One aspect of church life in the hills that is so special is the practice of the annual Memorial Meetings. There are hundreds of family burial plots scattered across the hills, and one Sunday out of the year, in summer or fall, each extended family will meet at their family graveyard for a preaching service and dinner on the grounds. It's a family reunion, memorial meeting and a church service, all in one.

Through the years we have attended and/or participated in meetings at Crochettsville, the Buck Herald Cemetery, two Turner family plots on Bowlings Creek, the Adams family, the Noble family and the Amis cemetery, where Wesley and I have reserved plots. The graveyards are always on a hilltop, sometimes difficult to get to, so you better park your car by the road and walk up. (I always marvel at how the hearse makes it up there!) Because the hill is rather rugged, the graves are scattered. On a flat spot a crude structure has been erected, a roofed over platform for this occasion, for the preachers. The congregation sits on planks resting on cement blocks under the trees. There is a box of newspapers handy, you grab one to sit on and one to fan with. There are huge maple trees for shade. A cemetery is a melancholy, peaceful place. Sitting there with our country friends, it is easy to feel like community and remember departed loved ones. And it's easy to worship. There is singing and powerful Bible-based preaching by uneducated, unpaid, Spirit-filled men—usually four or five preachers of various denominations, sometimes more.

Then it's time to eat. Tables are fashioned on the spot and quickly filled. Food was kept in coolers and cookers and boxes on the back of pick-up trucks until serving time. Food is bountiful and incredibly delicious. All women bring the best of their best to Memorial Meetings. They cook all day for several days early and late. Fried chicken, ham, chicken and dumplings, those often take center stage. All sorts of beans, potato salads of all descriptions, casseroles and salads, some traditional, some new. Desserts cover one whole table. A favorite is apple hand pies and there are never any left.

We are blessed to be a part of this culture, and I'm blessed to be a Mountain Preacher's Wife.

This was a speech given at Sunrise Chapel in 2002.

Fire at the Church

In 1954, while working the night shift at Whitfield, the Mississippi State Hospital in Jackson, Wesley bought an old manual Royal typewriter and a book of instructions: *Learn To Type in 24 Hours.* When the patients were quiet and asleep, Wesley set up the typewriter on an old metal table in the office and learned to type—somewhat. That old typewriter served us well for many years.

New Moon Over Slick Rock Hollow 149

The following letter was typed, with several carbon sheets inserted, to make extra copies.

Altro, KY
Feb. 5, 1961

Dear Folks at home:

Greetings to you in the name of the All Sufficient and All Powerful One. This greeting takes on new meaning to me tonight as I know He is able to do that which we are not able to do ourselves. The incident I will relate forthwith.

But for the miracle of God from Heaven in answer to our frantic pleas and some faithful neighbors and a passerby, tonight the church house on Bowlings Creek would be no more. It caught fire this morning after church and we thought all was lost. All we could do was pray and try to get to the place where the fire was. The water hose was frozen shut and the fire was in between the chimney and the building, behind wall board and things so that it was hard to get to. Let me say before going further that the damage was not over $100.00 to $150.00. The biggest item being that I do not want to start fire in the furnace (coal) again till the chimney is rebuilt and placed away from the building a few inches.

These cold mornings we have to start the fire early in the church furnace and get it to be a rip roaring fire so that the building gets warm for church services. I tried starting fire the night before and that might have helped a little but in banking the fire it still gets so cold in there. This morning it was warm in there and even the benches were warm and it was nice. I don't know when it started burning, but I had left to take the people home. Masty's were going to be here for dinner and Mast had gone with me to their house and come along back with me again. I had been hurrying and driving pretty fast today cause I wanted to get back in time for dinner. (The trip takes an hour and 15 minutes) and as we get to the top of the bank behind the church I saw the smoke coming out the louver of the gable end and around the roof by the chimney.

  I says, "Mast, the church is on fire!" and stopped the bus right there and ran and he right on my heels. I didn't know what to do first. Martha and the others in the house had seen the smoke a few minutes before and Martha went out to see. When she opened the door at the end toward the house all she could see was a house full of smoke and flames at the front of the church. She closed the door quickly to keep out draft and ran to the house to tell the others, Fianna and Frances (Fianna's first Sunday in church since the baby), and then ran to the neighbors. Hargas and three of his boys came right away and also Harlan Cole happened to be coming down the creek just then and they carried water and had just started pouring when we got here.

  I tried to get up the steps to the attic, a bucket of water in my hand and Masty right on my heels. I never got further than the top of the steps. We had to turn back because of the smoke. It was choking. Then I ran in circles for a few seconds praying for help as I went. Also tried to collect myself. Guess I got a bit fussy as I started shouting and begging orders to the rest. Told them where to find the ax and also the ladder. We had to get to the fire from the outside and from the louver above where the fire was. We took the ax and chopped out the louver and poured water in here. I just begged for water and soon there were boys and people running to the house and to the creek for water and they brought it faster than I could chop holes into the building.

  Masty then took my post on the outside pouring in and I went inside to the front of the church and chopped out the wall board behind where we thought the fire was. After we got to the fire we could work on it and though it had burned 2x8 studding nearly in two and quite a bit of the wood sheeting the Lord helped us to get it out. A very few more precious minutes and the fire would have gotten to the pine upstairs rafters and that would have been the end.

New Moon Over Slick Rock Hollow 151

Martha remembered the two Carbon tetrachloride hand bulbs that we had and she had brought the one from the house. I had thrown that one in the worst blazing place and ran for the one we had in the church basement. It's a thing that you throw at the base of the flame and it gives off a fume that smothers the fire. They were given to us by Henry and Marie Zook. We hoped we would never need to use them but they were used today.

If it were not for this and if it were not for the other things to our advantage, we would have no more church building. Thanks to God's faithfulness. I am happy though that even fire cannot destroy the Church of Jesus Christ. Our Savior will be more precious to us as a group of believers here on Bowlings Creek because this day, Feb. 5, 1961. We had two definite answers to prayer that were nothing short of miracles. The fire was one, and I'll relate the other.

The bill for the Sunday School papers was due at Scottdale. This runs in the $80.00 for one year and there was only $34.00 in the Sunday School treasury. I had asked the congregation what they want to do. Do we want to continue the papers? And if we do, do we want to drain the Sunday School fund. They agreed that we could and then where was the other $50.00 going to come from. (This was about two weeks ago.) We decided to make it a matter of prayer to God asking Him for $50.00. And this morning I was happy to tell them that the Lord had sent us the $50.00 to the penny.

We got the check in the mail this week from a family at Weavertown and they said in their letter, "Imagine getting a Christmas greeting and gift this long after Christmas," and listed some reasons and things why they didn't get the check here then. They didn't know that the Lord had His hand in all this and that He could use this family just at this very time to Glorify His Name in this way. It meant something to us as a congregation that the Lord undertook in this very definite way, and to the exact penny that we had asked for. Am telling you these things just for anyhow and to let you know that we are well and happy. My nose just started bleeding a bit ago.

Must have been from the burning in my nostrils from the smoke. Maybe it thinned my blood some or the tissues in the nose. It's stopped now and will be alright.

Thank you for your prayers for Kentucky, for us in the work and for the safekeeping of our lives. Today God has answered some of your prayers.

Check your stove pipes and chimney tonight before you go to bed and may God's lovely blessing rest upon all 'til we meet again. Who knows where or when, but may it always be in Peace.

Sincerely,
Wes and Martha

* * * *

The Flower Bed Story

Just outside our church door, there is a nice flower bed, with a story. . . .

Because of generations of isolation, mountain people tend to be suspicious of anyone not of their kind or from another hollow. At times, this resulted in feuds and long-time animosity. Communities and schools were plagued by cross-country angry competition and violence. Back in the fifties and sixties, organized church life was still rather new and the churches were not exempt from this deep-rooted prejudice. Our little church is situated close to the Breathitt County, Perry County line, and folks from both counties came to church. Sometimes they brought their prejudices with them. Wesley was very concerned about the situation and prayed much about it.

One day I suggested that space against the church wall could be made into a flower bed. He met the challenge and got to work.

"I drove over into Perry County and gathered up a pile of

New Moon Over Slick Rock Hollow

Wesley Stoltzfus and Paul Riley.

good solid sandstone rock from the roadside. Then I came back to Breathitt County and did the same thing. From that truck load of rocks I built a rock border for a flower bed. It was also a monument to our Lord Jesus Christ who is our peace and who makes us 'One.' In the center of the border I placed a large rock I found on the Breathitt-Perry line. On the upper side I cemented the rocks from Perry County and on the lower side the rocks from Breathitt County, praying all the while. When I finished, Martha saw a nice flower bed. I saw an altar of prayer and a monument of peace."

In the years since that, I have filled that bed with colorful summer annual flowers. They have never failed to provide a beautiful display. In the spring of 2003, Rhonda volunteered to plant the flowers. Steve found her there one day and told her the story of the flower bed. Rhonda took up the prayer challenge. The next day she and her son, Jordon, went back to the church to pray. She prayed for the Breathitt County people and for the Perry County people, and for the church, and for the man who built the rock wall.

Shortly before Wesley's death, Steve encouraged his Dad with this promise, "there will always be people praying for the church."

The spring following Wesley's death, Dan, the family horticulturist, planted several permanent plants among the annuals. There is a rose bush in the center, planted years ago in memory of Clifford Eash. Someone placed a "Garden Angel" at one end. In a simple ceremony, a plaque was placed there, in memory of Pastor Wesley Stoltzfus and his wife Martha. Now the rock-lined flower bed is a memory garden as well as an altar of prayer and a monument of peace.

- From *Hope in the Deepest Hollow* and an album by Fern Metzler

– CHAPTER 11 –

Decision Time

As an evangelist, Wesley often preached a series of sermons for revival meetings. During his preaching "career" he preached at scores of churches in Kentucky, Indiana, Ohio, Alabama, Michigan, Delaware, Pennsylvania, Iowa, and others. He would be gone a weekend, a week, or sometimes two. Invariably, in one of his sermons he included this story, the account of a spiritual experience at age 19.

One summer I sang bass in a male quartet. There was this Mennonite preacher who had a church in the heart of downtown Philadelphia. Regularly he conducted street meetings on a busy, noisy street corner. Melville Nafzinger was his name. Melville put out a plea for church groups in our area to participate. So that summer Steve, Mel, Vernon, and I, went to Philly once every week or so, to sing and testify at a street meeting.

That was fun. I enjoyed singing four-part men's songs. And because it took us several hours to travel from Lancaster to Philadelphia, I was free from farm chores for one evening. Everything was fine . . . until that preacher asked me to give a testimony. I had no testimony! I don't remember what I said, just mumbled something into the microphone and quoted a Bible verse—not loud enough to be heard above the roar of the overhead train. I was totally embarrassed and deflated. And the Lord began his convicting work on me.

I had been brought up in the church and in a godly family. In fact, I had been baptized and joined the church; it was the expected thing to do. At some point I had asked Jesus to forgive my sins, but, I had no relationship with the Lord. I was living my life the way Wes wanted to live it. "Sowing wild oats," we called it.

The following spring several singing groups met at Vernon's house, to organize and plan who sings what and which group goes when—that sort of thing. Again, I was part of a quartet, scheduled to participate in street meetings in Philly. I left that meeting and the convicting power of God went with me. I was a hypocrite and I knew it. I could not possibly engage in those Christian activities the way I was—something had to give.

I sensed that God not only wanted to forgive me, but also demanded to have **me**, my life, my allegiance. He desired to be my Lord. Somehow I knew this was my night of decision. I would decide to either yield to God's Lordship and follow His ways or I would turn and run and never look back.

If you had seen me drive home that night, you would not have believed it was Wes—he never drove that slowly! I moseyed along, chomping on an old cigar. I knew this thing must be settled tonight. Pulling into Dad's shed where I parked my 1942 Plymouth, I just sat there. I couldn't get out. I was fighting a life or death battle, and the struggle was intense. My Mother once told me, "Wes, there are two persons who fight for your life and soul—God and Satan. The battle is fought in your heart but you are the one who decides which one wins." I think I was afraid of what the Lord would ask of me if I followed Him. Be a preacher? No thanks!!

I don't know how long I sat there, arguing with the two voices. Finally, I just slumped over the steering wheel and prayed, "Lord, I'm yours! Do with me whatever, wherever, whenever. My decision is made. I quit fighting and yield to You and Your ways."

Since that night I have had many spiritual experiences and many spiritual struggles. Satan still desires to have me, as he wanted Peter. But I have never regretted the decision to give the Lord Jesus my life. I praise God for His convicting power, His saving power, His keeping power, and His guiding power. I gladly serve Him as Lord.

– *CHAPTER 12* –

Room 400

It was raining that September morning in 2002 as I walked across the street from my room at Kentucky Inn to Room 400, at the St. Joseph Hospital in Lexington. It was early, too early for clogged traffic on Waller Street, and I hurried. Sometimes Dr. Pierce arrived at Wesley's room before 7:30 and I wanted to be there. I slipped through the revolving doors into the lobby, past the coffee shop and the fountain that sprayed water incessantly. After three weeks, this part of the hospital was rather familiar. I pushed the "Up" button on the elevator and, once inside, the round "4." I hurried down the hall where the sign read, "Oncology," a grim reminder that this was no picnic. This morning, as always, I felt an urgency to hurry to Room 400, but now I was reluctant to push open the door. The door mutely shouted, "Please do not visit if you are ill. Wash your hands when you enter. Oxygen in use. No live plants." The familiar wheel of questions and fears began turning in my mind. *What will I find when I enter that room? Will Wesley be sicker or better? What will all the medical information register today? (The charts go down and up, along with my heart.) And the big question, why is my husband confined to Room 400 for five weeks? And, will he live? And how long? Or die?*

For a number of years, Wesley had been plagued with low blood counts that nothing would elevate. He often battled low-grade fatigue, and then, extreme fatigue, along with itching and infections on his legs and arms, and hives. His energy level lowered, but his ministry continued and life was good.

Then while we were living in Harlan, Indiana, for a short-term pastorate, several doctors in Fort Wayne came to a conclusive diagnosis: Acute Leukemia. We were devastated! Cancer! This happened only to other people, I thought. Cancer of the blood is serious stuff. That night in our trailer-home at the edge of Mart Graber's hayfield, in Harlan, Indiana, we held each other for a long time and cried. "There are still so many things I want to do, with you," Wesley said. His voice was muffled and tired.

"Like what?"

"I wanted for us to see the Canadian Rockies another time. And—my assignment here at Sunrise Chapel isn't completed." I knew what he meant. A year or so earlier when Wesley retired from the pastorate at Bowlings Creek, he had made another commitment to his Lord, "My life, whatever is left of it, is Yours. Do with me whatever. Send me wherever." Then had come the invitation to be Interim Pastor at Sunrise Chapel. We had been there four months.

Now this.

Gradually our devastation turned to hope. Hope for recovery. With hundreds of praying friends and with thousands of cancer drugs and treatments available, and with many competent doctors and nurses, surely this was not a death sentence. We knew the Lord has no limit to his healing abilities and surely Wesley's work isn't over. And, I'm not ready for life without Wesley. No way!

Events moved along rapidly after that. Wesley became very sick and spent several days in a Fort Wayne Hospital. Extensive treatment was recommended. Even though we had developed very strong love-ties to our friends at Sunrise Chapel, Wesley and I both experienced an intense desire to go "Home" for treatment. Home to Kentucky.

Now we were situated in Room 400 and were in the "waiting" mode; waiting daily for the results of the blood readings, waiting for the doctors' visits, eagerly waiting to see who would come to visit us, waiting for healing so "Life" could continue.

Quietly I pushed open the door and walked in. Even before I closed the door behind me, I heard his deep, strong voice, "Good morning, Sweetheart."

New Moon Over Slick Rock Hollow

I leaned over to kiss him, very carefully, since that sign on the door said no hugging or touching. "Good morning yourself. How was your night? How are you feeling?"

"I'm still 'high' on the experiences of last night." Ah yes, of course. Last night had been memorable. Many family members were in town, in and out of the hospital, in and out of Room 400. Wesley wanted everybody around. At one point our three sons were all there, reminiscing, telling stories, laughing. Then the singing began.

Steve wrote about it.

We three brothers decided to sing "Mansion over the Hill Top," the song that won for us the blue ribbon at a grade school Breathitt County Fair Competition! I think it was Mrs. Florence Deaton's idea, bless her heart. Anyhow, I wish you could have seen Dad's face. There we were, his three boys, at the foot of the bed with our arms around each other, with Mom and many of the rest of the family around. And there lay Dad in the bed, eyes closed, a big smile on his face, singing tenor as only Dad can—all rared back, throwing his head around like he does, and thoroughly enjoying himself. After the first verse, the rest of the family joined in and we had us an old fashioned singin'. Songs like: "The King Is Coming," (Remember when we sang that at grusmommy's sick bed at a Stoltzfus reunion?), "Beautiful Star of Bethlehem" (the last time we sang that together was at Eliza Cole's funeral), "We Have This Moment" (a favorite with Mom), and "Jesus, Tender Shep-

herd." (When we were children, Mom would sing us to sleep with that song and what a wonderful tucked-in feeling that was.)

At one point Mom, with tears, told of how it was to have the one you love the most stricken with cancer, and then how Dad would hold her and, sick as he was, comforted her. We sat there and cried with her and we all wanted a love like that.

It was getting late. Becky and I needed to leave and Dad needed some rest. Someone asked Dad if he would pray for his family and bless them. He prayed a beautiful heartfelt prayer thanking God for his wife and family and asking God's blessing on us. Forgive me, Dad, but I peeked during your prayer. What I saw is hard to put into words. Remember how Dad would often close the service at church? He would raise both hands up to God and out to his congregation and bless them. Now, picture this same man in a hospital bed on a cancer ward, flat on his back with his hair all gone, with both hands stretched up toward heaven and out toward his family. Picture his wife and children and children-in-laws gathered around his bed. Some kneeling at the foot of his bed, some crying and all of us being blessed. Comprehend if you can the tremendous blessing it is to have Godly parents like that.

"Now unto Him who is able to keep you from falling, and to present you faultless before the presence of His glory with exceeding

> *joy. To the only wise God our Savior, be glory and majesty, dominion and power, both now and forever. Amen."*
> *Then we sang "Eventide" and "God Be With You 'Til We Meet Again." Becky and I went home. I felt like I had been in Heaven.*
> *- Steve*

Now it was the morning after and breakfast arrived. "These cathead biscuits are pretty good, and I enjoy the oatmeal. How can anything so humble be so good?"

Dr. Pierce strode in, ever efficient but never too hurried. He looked somber. He told us, "Cancer strikes fear in the hearts of people. Leukemia strikes fear in my heart. Things look badly for you. Leukemia cells are very active. The blood counts stink. I don't know what to do next."

"So the chemotherapy and Lukine and all the other stuff hasn't worked?"

"No."

"But Dr., I'm feeling good. I don't know what the Lord still has up his sleeve for me."

"If you did know, you would know too much."

The doctor left and Wesley began singing.

> *When we get to Heaven with Jesus our King,*
> *We won't have to worry about anything.*
> *We'll be happy and free and our bodies will never be—*
> *Wore out!*

Marian and Faith arrived—all the way from Florida—to visit Brother and Uncle Wes. What an emotional reunion. It's so hard not to hug! Later in the day the door opened and in walked some friends from Sunrise Chapel. They were singing friends, and Fred carried a guitar and songbooks. Wesley picked up his harmonica, Fred began to strum, voices lifted in song, and the praise began!

> *There's a land that is fairer than day,*
> *and by faith we can see it afar.*
> *For the Father waits over the way,*
> *to prepare us a dwelling place there.*
> *In the Sweet By and By!*

Some of the nurses found excuses to check Wesley's vital signs, or his groshon, or whatever, just to see what's going on in Room 400. What *was* going on? We were having church with a few fellow travelers. We were shifting our focus from earth to Heaven.

Dave called. "What's with Dad? He is so euphoric!"

"I don't know. I guess it's like the Bible says, 'Though outwardly we are wasting away, yet inwardly we are being renewed.' (2 Corinthians 4:16) At this time it seems like your father is living on a higher spiritual level than the rest of us. His prayers and blessings are so powerful. His singing voice is as strong as ever. Thanks for calling, Dave. And thanks for coming last weekend, and for letting Lois stay to be Dad's nurse."

Indeed, singing was a hallmark of Wesley's stay in room 400, and of his entire illness. He sang to exercise his lungs—to clear the pneumonia and to bring down his fever. It worked! He sang to worship the Lord. He sang to testify of God's goodness. He sang to harmonize with others. He sang just because he loved to sing.

> *I Owe the Lord a Morning Song*
> *Through It All*
> *Someone to Go the Extra Mile*
> *Lord, Send Your Angels*
> *Blessed Assurance*
> *How Long? How Long?*

New Moon Over Slick Rock Hollow

Let the Blood of Calvary Speak For Me
I Will Glory In the Cross

And, of course, "Abide with Me," his evening prayer, every evening. Sometimes he fell asleep before he finished it.

"Are you tired?" I asked. Everyone had gone except Rosie, his private night nurse—one of his little girls.

"Yes, but it's a good tired." I laid my head on his chest, to cry, and to receive his blessing. He took my face in his big hands and we expressed our love for each other. The trek to my motel room was blurred. Back in Room 400, Rosie wrote,

> *Sleeping pill at 11:00. After the lights went out, I "blessed" him. I sat on the chair waiting for him to go to sleep. He sang his "Abide with Me" song, and then prayed out loud, first for Mom, then starting with Gerald and Fern, all the way to Keith and Lisa and their special unborn son. He mentioned everyone by name. He ended with, "Thine is the Kingdom, Power and Glory. Praise you Jesus. Praise you Jesus." And the next breath was a snore.*

Days and weeks passed. One night as I walked to my room, I spotted the new moon. I promised Wesley we would be at home when the moon was full. I was getting weary. Dr. Kennedy very kindly asked me, "And how are you feeling?"

"I'm feeling well."

"How can I say this kindly? You lie poorly," he said. I guess I was operating on God's grace. Annie Johnson Flint wrote, "When we have exhausted our store of endurance, when our strength has gone ere the day is half done, when we've reached the end of our hoarded resources, our Father's full giving has only begun."

We were thankful for God's "extra" blessings:

- *The children and in-laws who took their turns staying a night or two with their Dad.*
- *Wendy's shakes.*
- *Relief from nausea.*
- *McDonald's whatchamecallits from Christine.*
- *Several dozen blood donors. Also platelets donors.*
- *Care packages.*
- *Enough gift money to pay for my motel room for five weeks.*
- *Oncology nurses. They were all "keepers."*
- *A "boiled" harmonica to kill the germs, thanks to Carol.*
- *Christine's almost daily 5' 1" smile and "Blank" look.*
- *Becky's chocolates.*
- *Very little physical pain.*
- *Visits from our many good friends back home in Breathitt and Perry Counties.*

One morning in mid-October, Dr. Pierce sat on Wesley's bed and very candidly said what we already knew. "We have done all we can."

"To what would you attribute Dad's otherwise good health?" Gerald asked. Apparently Wesley's heart and lungs and other vital signs were in good shape.

"Wesley's faith and contentment, his family and his prayers," was Doctor's answer.

Wesley turned to me, "Honey, let's go home. I want to go home to Slick Rock Hollow in the worst way, home to Bowlings Creek. Whether to live or die, I don't know. I'm in God's hands.

Then he turned to Dr. Pierce, "When I was wheeled in here five weeks ago, I was told this would be my home for awhile. I looked at the four walls and thought I would go batty. But these have been some of the best times with my family and wife, in spite of cancer."

We made plans for Hospice care at home, and the girls stripped the room of piles of cards and posters and other well-wishing paraphernalia. Wesley was so excited; he nearly forgot he was sick. We said our thanks to the nurses and doctors. We were ready. Ready to leave Room 400 and begin another phase of life. Or death. I remember Wesley's prayer the day we left Room 400, "Lord, help my family keep a song through all this mess."

* * * *

Wesley did return home to Slick Rock Hollow. For several months he experienced a partial clinical remission of leukemia, several months of wonderful times with family and friends, a time of preparation for leaving here and entering There. He continued singing and praising and blessing, to the end. He died April 26, 2003. I know he is still singing and praising and blessing, in a Heavenly Realm.

– CHAPTER 13 –

Twilight, the Beginning

Twilight is brief. It serves to slow us down, to make us drowsy and prepare us for the night. As twilight deepens, we begin to shed the burdens and responsibilities of the day. *Everything will be better—come morning.*

When Wesley came home from the Lexington hospital, we realized he was entering the twilight zone. Not to worry; God is still in control! So we tried to prepare for the night. Several urgent matters needed his attention. He wanted to "do" a Jacob. Two by two, as the children came home, he called each of them and their families to him, laid his hands on them and prayed a blessing on each one. Sue remembers:

> *Dad took Bill and me, and our kids, into the bedroom, away from the rest, and told us how much he loved us, what he appreciated about us and then laid his hands on each of us and prayed a powerful prayer of commitment and of God's blessing on us.*

Something else needed attention before he could go. "Call Masty. Tell him and Fianna to come down; I want to talk to them." When they came, we cranked up his bed and he started talking. "I'll get right to the point. March 7th was 51 years that we have been in Kentucky. I have been reminiscing about all my friends and coworkers and I wanted to thank you for all the help you have been in spreading the gospel of Jesus Christ. *The pain is forgotten and the joy is paraded before my mind.* I'm remembering the Bible Schools at Otter Creek, at Gays Creek, and at Bowlings Creek." Prayers and tears were exchanged that evening. This scene was repeated either by visits, or by letters, with several other church friends.

Wesley was getting his house in order.

As Phil said at Wesley's funeral, "According to all medical expertise, Wesley was supposed to have died in November—it would have been a short time. Does God perform miracles? Is God a Healer? I believe God was ready to take Wesley Home. But I think Wesley asked a favor, 'Lord, there are a couple of things I would like to do. I would like to go home to Slick Rock Hollow with Martha. And I would like to see my new grandbaby, Lisa's Little Wesley, yet unborn.'"

"And God said, 'Sure, no problem. I can heal you and let you do those things before I take you Home. And I have a special bonus for you. I'll let you go to Florida to Ministers Fellowship Meeting and see all those ministers that you have worked with through the years.'"

Partial clinical remission is the medical term describing Wesley's next five months. I call it an extended Twilight, a divine healing.

The following are some excerpts of letters he wrote during that time. He never apologized for his poor spelling, which made his letters a fun challenge.

This letter was sent to Max Zook and the church conference family. Max did us a favor by editing the first draft!

Wesley, I sentr the following message to rthe CMC family. I edited yours. I hope irt is OK. See, my infured finfger keeps hittinfg the f and r when itr shouldn't. I understand your problem wirth the ssss. I will add you to the conference email list. - Max

Martha has been after me to do an update on the cancer deal that's going around in my body. There is not much to say except that I'm still alive. But if my health is no better than my typing, then I'm bad off. I have felt better today, probably than at any other time since we came back from the hospital. The fact that I have been feeling so good all this time is not exactly a mystery, but a wonderful gift of the amazing Grace of our Father in Heaven. Made possible by the Blood of Calvary, and conveyed to us personally by the Spirit of God. So, what I can say is that God is gracious. I'm at home with the Little Woman. There is fuel in the tank that runs the furnace, we have electric everywhere in the house, I'm retired with my feet propped up (mostly to keep the swelling down), have tons of friends who care and come to see us, pray for and with us. Special and honorable mention goes to our children and their spouses who have carried us through this time of whatever by just taking over and ministering to us through hands on demonstration of love, giving us hope and encouragement. Well, this is enough. I've sweat through enough. If you can't understand, call me and see if I can confuse you more gently.

- W. A.

To Cousin Betty whose husband had recently passed away with leukemia

Dear Cousin Betty, I have received the letter you sent and enjoyed hearing from you. And, yes, the grace of God is sufficient for each of us, and I'm sure that is the case for every new biggie we face, and, yes, you and I have faced some biggies recently. What is there from here on out????? Our Father knows, but I do not. I have experienced that He is there. My life takes on new perspective, and the same is true for Martha. I am sure it has been much harder for her than me—the suspense, the not knowing, and the many other demands on her spirit and time. . . . And after so long a time on

New Moon Over Slick Rock Hollow

Remember the good times with Papaw.

this comp. I cannot type or get it togewther . . . so . . . God bless you and keep you in His grace. When thou walkest through the waters . . . because He is there they shall not ore flow thee.

This letter was to our dear friend, Eula Swartz:

. . . I remember Bro. Alvin's preaching with tears of compassion running down his face. . . . Your own sweet smile and pleasant personality which you still have. I suppose, though, that Bro. Alvin preaches without tears in heaven or if he does, God stands there wiping them away, for He promised that they would be wiped away in Heaven . . . does that mean that there may be tears in Heaven but He keeps them wiped away????? That would be so much better than getting our grubby hands in our eyes.

But Eula, what does one do when at the lowest point you gather the preacher and your children around and make funeral arrangements . . . do a Jacob and bless each husband and wife team and then their children (the one, Lisa's baby in the womb), and then bounce back??? Martha and I, under the Lordship of Christ have had some quality and difficult times. . . . What is there yet for me?? Will I preach again??? work in the shop??? go to conference???

I did preach at a funeral for Lizzie Clutter who had told me that if I outlive her she wanted me to preach her funeral. . . . I did preach for about 15-20 minutes hard as I could go. . . . first time preaching since 8th of Sept. 2002. Somehow, preaching turns me on if it doesn't anyone else. . . . Visiting is also up there in the turn him on list.

I'm trying to learn a new song, an old Baptist type song. One line is "Jesus will forsake me never." When I get to that line I hump up and cry, and I can't sing and cry or preach and cry at the same time, as did your preaching husband. It will take me some time to get through that line without weeping. We have experienced that fact intensely in the last few months—I mean the never forsaking part—the weeping part, Martha and I have also experienced. May we ever be pliable in the Potter's loving hands. We are safe there, Eula. And I am mousing out . . . Ky. Stoltzfus—also known as Wesley.

To Family and Friends far and near:

This morning I puttered around the house awhile, started up the van to see would it, and run it for a spell—it hadn't been started or run since sometime Oct or Nov. Can't run it as we don't have any insurance on since I'm out of the shop. Just sat in it awhile, you know, felt good. Probably looked good. Reminded me of the man that said, "If a woman wants to look good—she goes to the hairdresser and to shop for a new dress and to the nail clinic to have her nails done, but, if a man wants to look good, he just goes and buys a new Bass Boat or an old pick-up truck and just sits in it!!!" Told Martha, I wish we had a load of furniture to go somewhere like Pennsylvania or Indiana or Alabama or Ohio like we used to. Always enjoyed those delivery trips with Martha. Always loaded to the gills and sometimes in the wintertime it was cold as kroute—not much heater in those old clunker vans. I checked the heater in the van this morning to see if it throws heat—not only did the front heater heat up but the back unit did to . . . what a pity we have heater now but no furniture. Cranked up the lawn mower too, to see if it goes in the snow—it doesn't, had to put it back in the shed.

. . . alright, there you got it, folks. Am still on low dose of Prednazone for a few days and am eating us back into the obese gray pretty dark area—plum disgusting. I may have to volunteer to go back on the peaches and watermelon diet when I couldn't eat anything else . . . enough of that kind of chatter. . . . Hallelujah for the healing that God has already given. Bless His wonderful name that I can even crawl—let alone go all over the place. No pain, no heavy responsibility bearing down on me to scare me, and Martha has been marvelous through this whole thing, and friends have held us up through prayer and more prayer, and visits and hundreds—right—hundreds of cards and notes. . . . I feel sorry for you if you been trapped into reading this whole miserable thing. Supper is near ready and I'm out of here—do your own spell checking . . . this was Wes, or W.A.

Wesley collected friends as some people collect trophies. Each friend was a trophy—a splendid variety of special people. Some were "characters." Erv is a "character" with a huge heart. Nearly every day during Wesley's illness and beyond, when we opened our mailbox, we found a postcard with a handwritten note, from friend Erv. I saved them all—there are over 200!

Here is Erv's reply to Wesley's letter.

Best wishes and thanks, Martha, for making W. A. take time to write. I haven't laughed so much for a long time. I can just see you, W. A., in that big empty van with both heaters blasting away, and thinking back when I and Beulah used to drive our 1952 old Chevy pickup with a live bred sow in the back bed with some straw, and take off for KY in the middle of the night and head through all the curves and hills and get to Bowlings Creek 12 to 16 hours later. What a trip with our two children with us in the front seat, 'cause we didn't know what a crew cab was back then. God is good and we are thankful. Beulah's letters used to make me feel as good as this one does. Dock and Lizzie are doing pretty good—he still smokes a pack of cigs a day.

- Friend Erv

To quote Phil again:

Wesley ran the strong race. Then about eight months ago, it appeared that he was getting ready to finish his race when he was diagnosed with leukemia. If we would have had his funeral back then, we could have said he had run a good race. But in the last eight months God had given him, we see not only a lifetime of a good race but we see a tremendous finish.

I coach cross-country racing and in that kind of running we talk about the "sprint line," when the runner is within sight of the finish line. We try to teach the runners that at the point they see the finish line, and know that's where they are going, to give it all they've got. I believe Wesley, spiritually speaking, sprinted to the finish line.

God enlarged Wesley's ministry of encouragement in those last months, especially his gifts of songs and prayers. It was one of those times that Wesley needed a blood transfusion. Rosie and I took him to the Jackson Hospital and parked at the front door. With cane in hand, he slowly started for the door.

"Wesley, wait!" A young lady, quite distraught, came running up to us. "My son is here in the hospital, real bad off. Please pray for him!"

So he did. He was so weak he could barely walk, but he found strength to stand in that parking lot and pray for this needy mother and her sick son. I didn't speak my angry thoughts. *Can't you see this man is sick too? He is the one who needs prayers and care....* A compassionate heart ministers beyond personal pain.

Before his illness, there were often several "key" people in Wesley's life. He prayed for them and with them. He deliberately planned to connect with them to encourage them. I called these people his "projects." At one time his projects were Levi Combs, Uncle John Blank, and Jesse Cole. Every week or so he would say, "I need to visit Uncle John," or Jesse, or Levi. And always he had an intense burden for pastors, both in Eastern Kentucky and the larger church. He knew from experience the wonderful challenge of being a Shepherd. He knew also the burdens, the temptations and discouragement that accompany that calling. So he made an effort to encourage and to pray.

Jesus said, "Give and it will be given to you. A good measure, pressed down, shaken together and running over, will be poured out to you." Our friends were glad to give back to Wesley some of what he had poured out to them: letters, cards, phone calls, visits, gifts, food, blood, prayers, kind words, laughter—all were tokens of love and encouragement; gingerbread, chicken 'n dumplings, with plenty of "Yeller sop," were all received with thanksgiving. In a somber sick room, we were desperate for laughter, so we enjoyed the funny cards and jokes. Then there was the practical help: somebody checked the oil in the Buick and someone else ordered fuel oil and installed an A.C. unit for the house.

Give me the flowers while I live,
Trying to cheer me on.

Useless the flowers that you give,
After the soul is gone.

Wesley and I had bonded in a surprising way with the people at Sunrise Chapel in Fort Wayne, Indiana. Here is part of a letter Wesley wrote to Craig and Cristal and family.

Just this yet . . . been sitting here remembering your family—great memories. Kay—testing the pre-adult waters with her parents, Mor—I can see those serious eyes and sense inner strength, J.D.—the middleman between two girls, and two girls. I also was a middle child—a key place—and I can still see Noah at the back of the trailer coming on the four-wheeler, with a cantaloupe in his arm for me, at a time when that, plus peaches, was about all I could eat—and how good it was. And Jed—I see you leaning on the edge of the bed at Ft. Wayne hospital talking to me—friend to friend—and I wish I could hold your face between my hands and look deep into your eyes and say, howdy, Jed—it would be enough.

Memories are great, but its the people in the memories that we are so grateful for—the people at Sunrise have made a profound impact on our lives, also our children. Thank you.
                                                                                - Wes Stoltzfus

It was midnight. From my bedroom I heard the little bell tinkle at Wesley's hospital bed in the living room. Immediately I heard Becky rise up from her sofa bed and whisper, "How can I help you?" Steve was on duty also, asleep on the floor. Several hours later they had to drive back to Morgan County for work. This scene was replayed dozens of times. Twila left her family in Pennsylvania to spend a week with us. Lois and Sue and Carol did the same. Gerald and Fern came from Alabama many times. Lisa couldn't help very much because of her swollen belly and swollen ankles. Rosie spent many days and nights here. They ALL helped. Such was the support of family.

New Moon Over Slick Rock Hollow

Rosie wrote this:

"*Mom and Dad are watching* Fiddler on the Roof. *It may be a late night! When I got here Dad had just finished his bath. He told me he feels so good he could dance a jig if he could balance on one foot! He did a little jig anyway. I do believe he feels better every day. It continues to amaze/baffle me! Dad ate two plates full of Phil's supper. He even ate mashed potatoes. In the hospital he had vowed he could never again look a mashed potato in the eye!*"

I remember writing this in December.

This morning I wished to be a photographer. Every twig and weed had a ridge of ice and every berry had a drop of ice. When the sun hit, it all turned to crystal. Beautiful!! Then I would have brought the camera into the kitchen and . . . no, a camera can't record the aroma of coffee brewing and mush frying. Then I needed a tape recorder to record Wesley and his harmonica:

Be still, my soul, the Lord is on thy side,
Bear patiently the cross of grief or pain . . .

I got the hymnbook out and we sang the whole song (when I wasn't crying).

Be still my soul, the hour is hastening on,
When we shall be forever with the Lord.

Next he played:

In dem Himmel ist ruh. In dem Himmel ist ruh.
(There is sweet rest in Heaven.)"

— Mom

In February after two wonderful weeks with friends, and sister Marian in Sarasota, Florida, Wesley's strength and health began to decline noticeably. We had some sad, sweet, and scary experiences. We made several trips by ambulance to our local hospital for blood transfusions.

"Come here, Sweetheart, let me look at you." I moved closer to Wesley's bed at the Jackson Hospital. He looked me over and said, "I was afraid I would not be able to focus on your face again." Then he took my face in his big hands and said, "I love you. I think I have always loved you . . . and your children and grandchildren." He paused. "I will love you 'til death do us part." Another pause. "I don't want to leave you, but I may not have a choice." Then he released me and began to sing, *I don't regret a mile I've traveled with the Lord.* And . . . *Hold on, my child, joy comes in the morning.* Then . . . *It is better Farther on.*

I went on home to rest, and left the girls there at the hospital with their Dad. I should have stayed. He missed me. So he called me on the phone, said he just wanted to hear my voice, and we cried together.

April 26, 2003

Wesley's grandmother clock was standing in the corner of the living room, ticking out his last minutes. It quietly chimed out the hourly time, then struck 1-2-3-4-5-6-7-8-9-10. (Ever after this, at 10 o'clock, Saturday morning, I remember this scene.) I try to forget the seizures, the chills, the restlessness, and hard breathing. I remember the sweet drama of those last hours.

Most of the family was there or getting there. Twila insisted on singing, of all things, "You Are My Sunshine!" Kim, the Hospice nurse, came to be with us. Fern was talking love-talk with her Daddy. Becky and Sue were doing their usual practical nurse care things. Rhonda came to take Twila's boys to her house. Bev sat beside Wesley,

New Moon Over Slick Rock Hollow

briefly, and stroked his arm. We sang "A Wonderful Savior is Jesus My Lord." Dave added the bass in place of his Dad's. We all expressed our love and prayed. He was alert and communicated with his eyes. No words. Then . . . he prayed in a mumbled but clear voice:

> *Dear Heavenly Father*
> *This body has gone as far as it can.*
> *Ashes to ashes . . . dust to dust.*

He had prayed the committal prayer for himself that he had prayed at dozens of funerals. Then . . . "With groanings that cannot be uttered," he prayed for me and for our family.

I took Wesley's hand and prayed, "Lord Jesus, I'm holding Wesley's hand. Now you take his hand and lead him across the Jordan, so he can see you face to face. It will be alright then. Thanks for being with us here in this 'Parting.'"

His breathing slowed. He raised his arm, opened his eyes, wide, and looked at me. No, not *at* me, but *past* me. His gaze went beyond us, past the window and the hills . . . then, with a glimpse into Eternity, his face relaxed and he was gone.

> *From Light to Dark*
> *From Dark to Light.*

Steve stopped the swinging pendulum on the clock. It was 10:26 a.m., April 26, 2003.

Weeks later, when I browsed through Wesley's collection of old songbooks, I found his well-worn copy of *Coleman's Songs for Men*, published 1932. Inside the cover was written:

> *W.A. Stoltzfus*
> *Lancaster R5*
> *Pa.*

Leafing through the browned pages, I remembered when I was just getting acquainted with Wesley, he was already singing. He and his singing buddies would "hang out" and sing—male quartets, male chorus, mixed chorus. Voices came back to me and I could hear them sing, "Wonderful Story of Love," "Great God of Wonders" (this one has a wonderful bass run), "The Wayside Cross," "My Anchor Holds," "Sail On!," "Day is Dying in the West," and many more. My tears were falling on the pages when I found this one:

Twilight is falling over the sea,
Shadows are stealing dark on the lea,
Born on the night-winds, voices of yore
Come from that far off shore.

Chorus:
Far away beyond the star-lit skies,
Where the love light never never dies,
Gleameth a mansion, filled with delight,
Sweet happy home so bright.

Voices of loved ones, songs of the past
Still linger round me while life shall last,
Lonely I wander, sadly I roam,
Seeking that far off home.

– CHAPTER 14 –

He Bottles Our Tears

After Wesley's death, my feelings asked to be recorded, so I did some journaling. It was an outlet for my grief and a way to express some outrageous emotions. Like the Psalmist David, I was brutally honest; so perhaps some of my journal entries won't sound "healthy" or even "Christian." But that's the way it was. The exercise, I think, helped in the healing process. If, by revealing some of my intense struggles, I can encourage someone else to walk with the Lord through the Valley of the Shadow of Death and into the Land of the Living, I will be grateful.

April 30, 2003
The heart has gone out of my life. It lies crushed and broken. Will I ever again enjoy life? My life responsibilities are finished. I had two God-given tasks: to raise our family and to be Wesley's helper. Our children are all grown and capable of caring for themselves. And now Wesley doesn't need me anymore. Is this the end? I have only one reason to step into another tomorrow; so God can manifest His grace to this one desperate child. God will prove to Satan, and to anyone else who may be watching, that *He is enough*.

Early May
The actuality of this complete separation hits me again. The realm of life that Wesley is realizing and living is totally separate from my life—no communication between the two. I am here and he

is there—and he won't be back. Our union was so close. How can I possibly function outside that union?

May 3

It's Saturday again. He has been gone a week.
And he hasn't come back.
He won't be back.
I would answer the phone, "Hello," or "Good Morning."
"W. A. here. I'm in Jackson on my way home. Do you need anything from town?"
"No, just come on home."
"I'll be there."
I would begin looking for him in about 40 minutes.
But, he hasn't called.
His car is here, but he isn't.
He won't be back.
Ever.
Never.

Has he forgotten that he was ever here? Does he know that I miss him and that I'm grieving? I think of him constantly. Does he ever think about me? We were together constantly—emotionally and physically. Now he is there and I am here and our relationship is severed.

May 5

I walked up the road to see Bell. I hadn't seen her since Wesley got sick. I told her of Wesley's death. No one had told her. In that dark, drab little house, she and I grieved together. We cried together a long time. She grieved for Wesley and for her Levi.

"He was the best friend we had."
"So close and I didn't know he died."
"He wasn't real old."

"Where did you bury him? Didn't he want to be buried with his people, where he grew up?"

Belle continued, "When they's gone, hits never the same– and they don't come back. Do you stay by yourself? You never git over it. Least I don't. If hit's the Lord's will you kin stay by yourself. You have your chillun and young 'uns. I hain't got nobody. I swear, I hain't heerd about Wesley! When did you say it happened? Was he sick long? Hit's never the same again. Levi and Mam and Lizzie are all at the Combs cemetery."

I was talking with someone who understood.

May 17

It's Saturday morning again. Wesley's grandmother clock is ticking and chiming. It's been three weeks ago that Steve stopped the clock at 10:00 a.m., because Wesley left us. One minute he was here, the next moment—gone. Where? To his Eternal Home. Really? Are you sure? Yes! Yes! What is he doing now? I wish I knew. Does he know what I'm doing—cleaning the church, writing thank you notes to people who gave us money for his funeral? I don't think so. People say, "How are you doing?" Sometimes I don't think I will ever be able to make it. Every time I wake up in the night or in the morning, my split second first thought is, "He is gone!" Then I reach my hand over to where he used to lay beside me in bed. And I cry.

In all their distress He too was distressed. Isaiah 63:9

Lord, do You hurt when I hurt?

Do You cry when I cry?

Are You in anguish when I am in anguish?

I'm so thankful that my spiritual condition doesn't depend on my feelings. My relationship with Jesus doesn't depend on how I feel; because how I feel now is betrayed, rejected, forsaken, broken, alone. In my body I feel exhausted, bone weary, like a physical force is pushing against my chest. Some say they *feel* the prayers of God's people, they *feel* the everlasting arms of Jesus holding them. I have felt none of that. But that doesn't mean He isn't here. By faith I *know* His strong arms are holding me. Though I feel no joy, I *know* His Joy is my strength. I *know* every prayer for us is answered or will be answered. Is it possible to experience the presence of God without feeling it? Yes!! I praise God that all His promises are true, regardless of how I feel.

May 18

Sunday. It's been three weeks. This is the first Sunday I went to church by myself. I wondered where I would sit. The few times Wesley and I went together after Indiana, we sat just behind Masty and Fianna, where he could "hear good." No one else sits on that bench. Would I sit alone? I was just sitting down when Shirley and little Rebecca followed me, and sat down. Bless Shirley's heart. Then we had a carry-in dinner for Ruth Yoder. It wasn't the same without Wesley. I looked for him everywhere; going through the food line, piling his plate, chatting with P.R. and everyone, thanking the cooks, encouraging the kids. . . .

May 21

Lord, all I see out there ahead is endless, empty days.
Empty of Wesley.
Empty of meaningful activities.
Endless lonely.
I don't want to be alone. I don't want to be with anybody, only Wesley.
My days ahead seem empty of everything except GOD. God, are you enough? Yes, God, you are enough! Holy Spirit, teach me that God is enough.

May 22

Sometimes this grief is a physical pain. I was walking up to the mailbox. Something hit me in my chest, so hard I nearly staggered! It was raw grief—a physical thing.

May 27
Now it's been a month. I am still distraught, but I have no doubt that my God is within, at work. Otherwise, I would be destroyed. If I dare look beyond today, I see only an endless road of aloneness and no purpose for life. What will I do? Who am I? Before, I was Wesley's wife, doing what he was doing, more recently, caring for him. Now . . . ?

May 29
"Bear" Noble is a big overgrown young man from Bethel Camp. The other day I pulled into Wal-Mart. Across the way, Bear pulled in. Some people are embarrassed when they see me. Should they talk to me or turn and go the other way? If they do talk to me, should they just say, "How are you?" or mention this "thing" that has happened to me? Bear had none of those questions. He walked over to my car, I opened the window, and he reached his big arms through the window and gave me a big "Bear" hug.
"How are you?" he asked.
"I'm O.K."
"How are things going *really*?" So I told him.

* * * *

Jasper, the mail carrier, drove to the house with a package.
"How are you doing?"
"Pretty good."
"Lonely, though, I guess."
"Yes, very."
"Do you stay by yourself, Mrs. Stoltzfus?"
"Yes, but the children are in and out."
People care, I know. Even the mailman. I wonder what Jasper thinks about all the mail I get—219 cards, so far, besides packages.

Undated. It could have been anytime and always.
If possible, I would resign from widowhood. However, my trials fit me. They are custom made, just for me, by One who knows exactly how to arrange everything in my life for His glory and my good.

So, even though I don't like it—I hate it—yet, I decide to doggedly and joyfully (Is that a contradiction?) receive from my Heavenly Daddy, my widowhood.

May 31

Dear Wesley,

Rosie offered to take me along to Laura's high school graduation yesterday. Since you couldn't take me, I accepted the offer. It was a typical county high school graduation. However, it was very special because it was Laura Beth. She is a beautiful girl and so sweet. She got lots of honors and made us all proud. The whole evening was extremely difficult because you weren't with us!! I didn't know it would hurt so much. Will it always hurt, until I see you again? I'm so glad you are experiencing *Fullness of Joy*!

- Martha. IGD.

June 2

It's been over five weeks since Wesley is gone. I thought perhaps I should be doing a little better. Instead, last night I awoke after having slept several hours. Suddenly I felt so utterly devastated, such excruciating pain, so forsaken and abandoned, such agony of spirit, that I wept and wailed for a long time.

Oh Lord, how long until You come to me with comfort and rest?

God understands. I embrace the suffering—again.

Eventually the Lord will give me a song in the night and joy in the morning.

June 7

Dearest Wesley,

I just read a love note you wrote for me on Valentine's Day of this year (2 months ago), expressing your deep love and appreciation for me. I wonder, *how do you love me now? I mean, if you wrote a note to me today, what would it say?* I'm too earthy to know. I love you.

- Martha. IGD.

June 10

It's as though Wesley has fallen off the face of the earth (or rather, flown), and nobody is looking for him. He left no forwarding address. Nobody asks, "Where's Wesley?" They hardly mention his name. Used to, wherever I went, people would ask, "How's Wesley?" No more. It's like he never lived here.

June 11

Dearest Wesley,

Somehow I feel rejected, forsaken, abandoned. You left me and I couldn't go along. There is no way to reach you now. Why did you do that to us? You are in a time and place so utterly separate and foreign to me. And you don't need me anymore. But I need you! When are you coming home?

- Martha

June 12

I'm an old woman and my husband is dead. So what does it matter how I look or how I smell? So what if I get dumpy fat and my clothes don't fit? What if my teeth all fall out and my hair is in disarray? Yet, surprisingly, I do take showers and shampoos. I check the scales and I even bought a new dress. Of course, I'm just following my life-long habits. But I think it's more than that—it's Jesus in me, motivating me to still be "nice."

June 13

Early on, I often thought the question, "Is Wesley *really* in the presence of Jesus *now*? Really?" For some reason, I blurted out the question to Mike Tabor, on the night of Wesley's funeral. He answered with a Bible quote, "To be absent from the body is to be present with the Lord." I was satisfied.

Perhaps soon I can stop wishing for Wesley to be here and start wishing for me to be there.

In your unfailing love you will lead the people you have redeemed. In your strength you will guide them to your Holy Dwelling. You will bring them in and plant them on the mountain of your inheritance." Exodus 15:13 (the song of Moses and Miriam)

Oh my Lord, that promise has already come true for Wesley. Someday you will do that for me also.

June 17

"I wonder if the choir in Heaven has noticed the increased richness in the songs these days . . . but here on earth the silence is deafening."

- Brenda Zook, in a card she sent me.

Thanks, Brenda, that says it so well!

June 18

Perhaps I shouldn't, but I do. I play the game of "Never Again."

Never again will I stew pretzels for Wesley. Or fix grits. Or buy gingersnaps and peanuts at the Dollar Store.

Never again will he deep-fry gallons of sweet potato chips. We will never travel to the Canadian Rockies together, just he and I. We won't ever again pick elderberries for jam and I certainly won't make pickled cantaloupes—he was the only one who ate them.

Never again will he and I snuggle as lovers. Neither will we load up the brown Ford van and trailer with a newly crafted walnut or cherry bedroom suite or various other pieces, to deliver to customers in Ohio, Indiana, Pennsylvania, or Alabama. That was such fun. Never again.

Never again will I be a preacher's wife. We won't go to Ministers Fellowship or entertain evangelists. He won't be having revival meetings anymore—anywhere, or weekend meetings or preaching at Memorial Meetings or funerals. Wesley's name will be deleted from the CMC directory of ministers. I will be in a widow's circle instead of a preacher's circle.

Never again will I hear his strong vibrant voice singing with a congregation—first the melody, then bass, then tenor. I miss his songs at funerals: "The Wayfaring Stranger" or "Palms of Victory," or "Zion's Hill." Or, "The Night before Easter," at a revival meeting after preaching about Christ's death and resurrection.

Never again will we have fun, together, with our many friends—traveling, visiting. Many of our friends are "couple" friends, and Wesley was the life of the party, the reason why we had such good times with our friends.

Never again will anyone hear his stories. He was a terrific storyteller, keeping the attention of a few or a crowded auditorium, with his real-life stories. Never again will he preach a powerful, Spirit-inspired sermon or lesson. I won't see him at his desk with his open Bible, preparing for a sermon. He used few "helps" and wrote very sketchy sermon notes—often only a few scribbled phrases and Bible references on a sticky note, stuck inside his Bible.

Never again.

June 21

The clock is striking 10:00 a.m. It's Saturday again, eight weeks later.

I didn't want to get up this morning.

I just want to go Home, with Wesley.

Rosie stopped in this evening. She was crying. We cried together, and talked about her Dad.

June 23

My faith in a sovereign God is secure. That fact does not protect my mind and emotions from some frightening questions:

Is the rest of my life worth living?

Is it worth the effort to come back to the land of the living—zestfully?

At my age?

Is Heaven real? The beautiful, secure, restful place in our imaginations—is that the *Real* Heaven?

June 24

"You will have a renewed passion in your soul, with a fire-tested awareness of the immeasurable value of one irreplaceable person."

- Billy Sprague, from *Letter to a Grieving Heart*

We are not indispensable, but we are irreplaceable!

The world, including Bowlings Creek, will go on without Wesley. But . . . there will never be another man to replace him.

* * * *

Today I went to Bithia Riley's funeral.

I imagined this scene in Heaven: Wesley sees Bithia for the first time. "Well, hello Bithia, my friend! You made it Home. Praise to Jesus. Since I can't officiate at your funeral, as formerly planned, and since you can't be at your own funeral, let's have a celebration here. Jesus will officiate, all the angels will be the singers, and you can testify how you got to Heaven by the mercy and grace of God, and I will sing:

I saw a way worn Pilgrim . . .
Shouting as she entered . . .
Deliverance *has come!*"

June 25
My faith has found a resting place. Period.
But my faith does not reach beyond today. I cannot see:
Joy in the morning.
A Spacious Place.
A Garment of Praise.
A Balm in Gilead.
Light after Darkness.
Renewed Strength.
A Song in the Night.
Morn shall Tearless be.
My faith is in God. That is enough. His promises will fruit. How, or when, or where, or why . . . I know not.

June 29
Sometimes I talk to Wesley. Most people think that isn't crazy. It doesn't seem farther out than talking to myself. Come to think of it, I don't remember reading about it in any of my "grief" books, as a normal means of recovery. It's normal for me. Becky said that Steve sings for his Dad when he visits the grave. And Sarah.

July 3
A new moon again. Changes.
The first call of the Whippoorwill.
The Summer solstice.
Fresh garden produce.
The first red tomato.
Day Lilies are blooming.
New things.
Roses will bloom again.

Everything is changing except my cold heart. Perhaps a little. Back in April the flowers and birds tried their best to make me happy. I'm afraid I disappointed them. I dare not disappoint my grandchildren. They don't like to see me sad. When they come, I'm happy. Or at least pretend.

July 12

It's Saturday again. Eleven weeks.

I glance at his grandmother clock and remember again. I recalled the death scene. As he stopped breathing, his eyes opened wide and looked past us, to Regions Beyond. And his face, I can't describe this, but his countenance changed—for just a few seconds his face became more alive and his mouth rested, almost smiled. Then his face and body relaxed. Somebody closed his eyes, and he was gone—at peace. His body was warm for a long time, and I placed my hand under his big hand one more time. It was still warm, but he did not squeeze my hand. He was gone. I removed my hand from his hand. I didn't want to feel the life leave.

July 13

Dave is here these two weeks to begin the process of liquidating Wesley's shop equipment and supplies. I was not prepared for the emotional upheaval!

Wesley was a pastor.

Wesley was a craftsman.

None of his handmade furniture is out there in the shop anymore except my casket and a cherry cedar chest with a scratch on the lid. He never sold anything that wasn't perfect.

Wesley was so pleased with his new shop that his many friends helped to build in 1993. He had many good years of work in that shop, creating fabulous and distinctive furniture—one-of-a kind—works of art. The memories are heart stoppers.

The smells: cedar, fresh shavings, lacquer, raw wood just planed.

The sounds: the saw, planer, and all the power tools that brought on his hearing loss, the stapler and lathe, classical music and Paul Harvey on the radio, rain on the tin roof, spray gun, and fans.

The sights: Wesley everywhere, pushing lumber through the planer, pushing panels through the sander. An empty coffee cup. His intense focus when applying the last coat of lacquer to a bedstead or cedar chest, with a mask on his face and a red kerchief around his forehead. *This is the last step. I must do it right!* I can see him standing beside a finished product, a satisfied creator, waiting my approval.

And now it's all over.

All the nails and screws, the casket hardware, the paint and sandpaper, the patterns and staple guns, and screwdrivers—all are sorted and laid out, ready to be sold to the highest bidder. Why must it be this way? Why can't Wesley and his shop go on forever?

It was hard on Dave too. He found all kinds of homemade "gizmos" and tinkerings and contraptions his Dad had made, to make his work easier. The drum sander is a classic. There was also a custom-made lazy susan multi-layered "thingee" with notches and holes and shelves and brackets to hold his small tools and supplies. It was always in the middle of his cluttered work bench. After Dave had cleared the work table he just leaned on that contraption a long time and grieved. "This," he said, "is Dad's tombstone. This is what Dad was."

At that point I had to leave the shop and cry. Then it seemed I heard Wesley say, *It's alright, Sweetheart. It's alright. Don't cry. I don't need that stuff anymore.*

Then I heard Jesus say, "It's alright, my child, it's alright. That shop was my gift to Wesley. But now I have something eternally better. Just wait and see."

I'm waiting.

July 14

Dear Wesley,

I like to create this picture in my mind, and I re-create it many times:

April 26, 2003, that morning when Heaven's gates were opened just for you, and you entered the realm of forever. A spirit-exploding, heaven-rending shout went up all over eternity—the voice of innumerable angels and millions of saints, shouting "Welcome Home, Wesley!" I see the banners and balloons and the smiles . . . they all know you! Trumpets are blasting, flowers strewn everywhere, fantastic heavenly parades, orchestras, choirs—just to welcome you Home! The echo reverberates from the mountains of Zion. But perhaps there isn't room for an echo—it's all real voices. Then the crowd separates and a royal carpet is rolled out, up to the throne. And there is Jesus! You are lost in His all consuming, all encompassing loving embrace.

And nothing else matters.

July 15

The lull in the storm, the brief reprieve from weeping I experienced a week or so ago, passed and the storm is back in full force.

I am weary of weeping, but I can't stop. My head aches, my eyes burn, and my stomach hurts. Still I weep.

Why doesn't somebody call?

July 19

Every night I listen for the first song of the katydid. I haven't heard any yet. Do they hesitate to start their chorus because it will make me sad? It will. It's just a reminder that the seasons pass—it isn't spring at all anymore, it's mid summer. I wish time would stop. I don't know why. Perhaps to keep these memories of Wesley vivid. I wish time would pass quickly, like the fast forward on a video, then I would soon be where I want to be—at Home with Wesley and Jesus.

July 20

It's Saturday night, and I'm sitting on the deck. It's been 12 weeks now. I feel dull. What can I say? The periods of weeping are just as intense, but less frequent. I guess it's true what Nanny (Combs) Turner told me the other day, "It gets better. If it didn't, we couldn't stand it."

I dread tomorrow. I dare not look ahead, it's a purposeless void. I wonder what Wesley is doing in Heaven tonight. Then I heard it! The first song of the katydid! I thanked the Lord for that gift and then went to bed.

July 21

Dear Wesley,

I miss you! I'm sitting at the picnic table with a cup of coffee. Jim Riley says our patio, on a summer morning, is an enchanted place. So it is . . . or was. Nothing is enchanting without you with me. The birds are feeding, the hummingbirds are in a frenzy, Chippy is searching for leftovers, and there are rabbits all over the place.

I miss you!

It's sweet corn time and I remember how you enjoyed corn on the cob. Sometimes you went to the kitchen, after your shower, for a bedtime snack. You wrapped two ears of corn in wet paper towels and zapped them in the microwave for several minutes.

I miss you!!

July 23

I am an emotional wreck. Last week I wept over the end of Wesley's shop. That was so much a part of who he was. This week I weep because not going to Conference marks the end of Wesley's life with CMC (Conservative Mennonite Conference) and RMM (Rosedale Mennonite Missions) and RBC (Rosedale Bible College). Wesley's involvement with those three organizations were also so much of who he was.

Now it's over.

July 24

I am weary of weeping. I am so tired of this endless mourning.

Lord, when will You come with Your healing? Why must it be so hard?

Lord, I am so tired. Help me!

Father, glorify Your name!

Lord, I trust these tears are not wasted. You are a God who specializes in redeeming impossible situations. Can You redeem my tears? Will I emerge refined?

And Lord, save me from self pity. I'm afraid of becoming obsessed with my grief. Help me!

August 7

The space between memories of the past and reality of the future seems to be widening, and I am sitting alone in this wide dusty desert.

August 9

The Renfro Valley trio sang the lonesomest song on their radio program . . . about the moon coming over the mountain and, "I'm sitting alone, with my memories of you."

So I did that.

The valley was already misty. The cardinal had sung his good night song in the crab apple tree and had gone to bed. Sitting on the deck, I saw the moon, just over the hill, orange like a slightly misshapen pumpkin. And I was alone with my memories of you.

Used to, when you were gone somewhere for the night, I would see the moon and think *Wesley can see the very same moon*, and feel connected somehow. Do you see this moon? Hardly. There is no sun in Heaven so there can't be a moon.

"And I hung my head and cried."

August 11

I was thinking, *Lisa's little children will never know their Papaw Wesley, and all the other grandchildren will finish growing up without their Papaw.* It's too sad to think about.

August 12

Dearest Wesley,

Yesterday Dock (Garfield) Deaton and his wife, Vergie, came to pick up his and Boyd's lumber they had stacked here, waiting for you to make more furniture for them. You and those Deaton men had an interesting relationship—they were your customers and friends. They are a rough and proud bunch with a tender heart, and they loved you.

After loading the lumber on his old beat-up pickup truck (he barely made it up the bank between the shop and shed, me and Vergie pushing and praying), I invited them to the house for a Pepsi. He roamed around, admiring our house and furniture that you had made, looking at your pictures and crying. And talking. He remembered all the furniture you ever made for his whole clan, and he is full of colorful local history and genealogy.

Garfield said, "Wesley liked it here, didn't he? He loved Bowlings Creek and never wanted to leave. You know, it's strange Wesley came here from 'off,' was it Pennsylvania? He settled here and had no desire to go back. Me, I was raised here, but I left when I was young, and I don't want to come back. I tried it once but it didn't work. It's strange. . . ."

I don't know . . . I think of the line in the song "You'll Never Leave Harlan Alive": "And you spend your life just thinkin' of how to get away."

I don't know. . . .

It's strange.

August 13

My emotions are real—
But not reliable.
They are felt—
But not trusted.
I can't deny my emotions,
Neither can they determine my spiritual state.
My emotions are very strong,
But they are fickle.
Sometimes I allow my emotions full reign—do whatever you want!
Other times I say to them, "Sit down and shut up!"
Sometimes I express my emotions,
Verbally or by pen or in prayer,
And God understands because that is part of who I am.
At times, by faith, I review and receive the facts,
And feelings are silent.

The facts are:
God is in control of my life.
He will never abandon me.
He will redeem my loneliness.
The Lord will complete the work He has begun in me.

August 18

I'm still waiting for morning. It seems mourning has come to stay.

I better wind Wesley's clock. It won't do for it to wind down.

August 20
I take a walk every day or two, about a mile. Since June 10 I have covered about 55 miles. By this time I should feel some extra endurance and energy. I don't. And I am still as dumpy as a cat-head biscuit. So what is the use? There is no purpose to life. Or meaning. So why write? Or sing? Or plan? Or cook? Or make a phone call? Or walk? Because I must do some things I don't feel like doing!

August 25
I haven't journaled much lately. I'm not sure why not. Perhaps it's because my thoughts and feelings don't look nice written down. Then I feel guilty, and I don't need false guilt mixed with all those other emotions.

I am convinced if it were not for my anchor in an all-loving, all-merciful, all-knowing God, and were it not for the prayers of God's people, on my behalf, I would be destroyed, emotionally and perhaps also spiritually and physically. As it is, I am merely exhausted, extremely sad, discouraged, and have no motivation or identity. I can't go on . . . but I must. I don't want to stay here alone, and I don't want to go anywhere else. I should be feeling positive and praising the Lord. I should be making plans as an individual "single" (ugh!!). I should be cooking nutritious meals for one. How do you make one serving of green beans and potatoes? Or lasagna? It's easier to lick a spoonful of peanut butter!

August 26
April—May—June—July—August. It's been 4 months.

"Wesley, it's been four months since you left. If you aren't coming back, you could at least call!" Then the phone rings, and for the second time today, there was no response at the other end.

"Hello?" Silence. "Hello. Anybody there?" Silence. Then the operator's voice, "If you want to make a call. . . ."

Perhaps he was trying to get through and couldn't.

August 28

This morning the humidity is down, and the air is clear after weeks of muggy foggy days. I feel better. Thank you Lord! I feel better!

August 29

Lord, you are wooing me from the jaws of distress to a Spacious Place, free from restriction. (Job 36:16)

But I'm not sure if I want that. It takes energy and courage to even want healing. It's easier to just sit here and rot! But Lord, You are wooing me. I'll get up and walk toward You, feebly. You say, "I'm working on your 'want-to' also." (Phil. 2:13) Lord, that is so good to know, because at times I don't want to do anything!

September 6

I came home at 6:00 after being gone for a week. I was alone, and had to carry my suitcases and "loot" into the house by myself. I walked all through the house, looking, checking. Finally, I opened the study door, thought Wesley might be in there.

He wasn't. I knew that, but still. . . .

September 8

While I was at Sue's house, one night I tried to go to sleep in Beth's bed. I was very tired and I told the Lord, "Lord, I'm too tired to talk with You, but it would be fine if You talked to me."

My Shepherd-Daddy answered with this lullaby:
> Sleep my child and peace attend thee;
> All through the night.
> Guardian Angels God will send thee;
> All through the night. . . .

I had not thought of that song for many years, but the words came back clearly. It was my Heavenly Parent singing!

I slept.

September 9

Dear Wesley,

Since I must live without you, I think I would rather be at home without you than anywhere else without you. I'm not sure. Crowds in an unfamiliar place are especially scary. I walked through the aisles at Wal-Mart in Archbold, Ohio, looking for you. And then, there was this big old man with a big belly, wearing a cap and suspenders. It wasn't you so I quickly turned and walked away, only to meet him again at the next corner. It was awful. In public places, unconsciously I'm looking for someone—you.

Home is a safe place.

I miss you, Wesley.

IGD.

September 10

"Lord, this pain, this grief, this darkness, is what You designed for me, because You love me. I see Your face looking into mine, with such love, pleading with me to understand this truth. So I relax in Your arms, and embrace the pain, because it is from Your nail-pierced hand. You put a lot of thought into this plan—the plan for my grief and loneliness and tears. Thank You Lord, for the pain; it is sweetened by Your love!" *The Lord disciplines those He loves.* (Hebrews 12:6)

September 13

Some people, when they cry, cry so prettily, with big tears trailing down their cheeks. My crying is not a pretty sight . . . my face scrunches up like a piece of wadded up newspaper left all night in the rain. And if I try to talk, my words come out all squeaky and unintelligible. Wesley always said he can't cry and preach at the same time. I can't either.

September 15

I feel emotionally dead. My life is colorless, drab. I didn't want to get up this morning. My morning coffee didn't help. About noon, the sun broke through, the humidity lifted. I felt some better.

Exactly a year ago today, Wesley was admitted to the hospital in Lexington, to be treated for leukemia. So many changes in one year! Everything has changed.

September 16

I bless the Lord, because He has redeemed my life from destruction.
I am troubled, sad,
distraught, weary, distressed,
cast down, disquieted, lonely,
heavy laden, frustrated, exhausted,
broken, worried, doubtful, bereaved,
hurt, anguished, mirthless, empty.
But not destroyed!
Bless the Lord, Oh my soul.

September 22

Lonely is a persistent, familiar presence. He follows me around the house, and sits beside me when I'm eating my sandwich. He is an obstruction when I pray and blurs my vision when I read. I beg him, "Leave me alone!" but he blatantly lies in my bed! After church, I watched Fern leave for Alabama. I came on home and Lonely followed me into the house.

"Lord Jesus, I invite You into my house. Abide with me and command Lonely to leave." Lonely doesn't stay forever.

September 25

This week is hard!
The other night I was sitting at the kitchen table in my night-

gown, eating stale Rice Krispies with spoiled milk. It was 2:00 a.m. In my mind I pictured Wesley opening the sliding door from the outside. He pushed aside the curtain and came in. He was wearing a long sleeved blue shirt with his dark suspenders and the cap that said "#1 DAD." In his hand he carried his worn brown briefcase and a nearly empty bag of Utz's hard sourdough pretzels. I knew he was back from a week-long 500-mile preaching trip. He looked at me, surprised. "What are you doing, still up this time of night? It's two o'clock!"

"I couldn't sleep," I told him, "because I had an hour long cry and you weren't here to hold me."

The picture faded. I dumped the rest of the soggy Rice Krispies into the garbage and went back to bed.

Late September

At times my emotions, my life, are like a raging torrent, out of control. Then again, I feel like a muddy stagnant pool, dead and lifeless, nothing but scum.

I wrote the above, stopped and looked at it. Then I remembered Ezekiel 47 and the awesome, mighty River of God—a picture of a life controlled by the Holy Spirit of Jesus! The Abundant Life!

"Father, I can't deny my feelings. At the same time, I acknowledge the facts: This River is so wide and deep, and originates from the Temple of God. It's a River of Delight, a River of Abundance. Abundance—large numbers, many kinds, all kinds, swarms. Whatever the River touches becomes fresh. Wherever the River flows, there is Life! Fruitful without fail!!!"

September 26

Jesus, I didn't know anyone could experience so much loneliness, I mean, I have always enjoyed solitude. But this loneliness is as different from solitude as day and night. To go out where there are people and activities, and to have people come to see me, eases the pain for a time. Then . . . I am alone again, and desperately lonely. The one person I am looking for is not here.

Lord Jesus, if it be possible, let this cup pass. If not, I will continue to drink the cup of loneliness. Lord Jesus, if it is possible, let your Awesome Presence abide with me and so replace this acute loneliness. Amen.

October 6

Dear Wesley,

Can you find my Dad today and tell him I still remember that October 6 is his birthday. If he were still with us here, he would be 123 years old. If you would count time by years over there, he would be 38 years old. But . . . you don't, so he is ageless, eternal. Just like you. Hardly a day passes that I don't wonder what you are doing today. I'm sorry, but I can only think in earth/time terms. Sometimes I ask God why he didn't take you and me together. I miss you dreadfully!

Your Sweetheart—Martha

October 7

The moon was coming in full. I went to bed but couldn't sleep. I cried into the night. Everything else was deathly quiet. Finally, when my tears were spent, I got out of bed, reached for my robe and walked out to the living room, without turning on any lights. I stopped. A brightness filled the room. Huge patches of light lay on the floor and illuminated my rocking chair by the window. It was the moon shining through our four-paned picture window, but it seemed ethereal. The moonlight and the chair beckoned me, but first I turned on the radio and discovered, "Music 'til Dawn" on WIJC radio. Beautiful, worshipful music filled the room. So I turned my rocker to face the moon, and propped my feet on the window ledge. I rocked and worshipped.

New Moon Over Slick Rock Hollow

Much later the moon diffused in fog and slipped behind the hill. I went to bed to sleep.

October 11

Dear Wesley,

It's a beautiful weekend in October and I would love to travel somewhere, with you. Fern and Gerald are in the Smoky Mountains with the Metzler family. Phil and Rosie are on an overnight retreat to Cumberland Falls. Steve and Becky are on a motorcycle trip to Columbus, to visit Keith and Lisa. Bill and Sue went on a bike trip the other week. P.R. and Bev are in Tennessee for a visit. Mast and Fianna are planning a trip to Lancaster County. If you were still here, you and I would go somewhere too. Either to a preaching assignment or to the Smokies or to visit our children. That was one of our "together" pleasures. You enjoyed driving and I enjoyed the scenery and just being with you. We both enjoyed eating at Shoneys, or wherever. And truckers' coffee if you got sleepy.

Sometimes we sang together or listened to tapes. If you were on your way to a preaching place, you would listen to S. M. Lockridge's sermon "Amen!" You had some of it memorized. When the way got long and tiring, we would listen to Dolly Parton's "Heart Songs." (If I listened to that now, I would cry.) Then you would lay your big hand on my arm and say, "Getting tired, Sweetheart? Why don't you lay back and rest awhile?" Thanks to you insisting that our cars all had a reclining seat on the passenger's side, I could do that. Then you listened to classical music on NPR radio.

I miss you still, very much, Wesley, and I miss our trip times together. Perhaps we can travel together again, in the Heavenly Realm.

Until death did us part,
Your Martha

October 15

Last week Sue sent me this book, *Tear Soup—A Recipe for Healing After Loss*. It's a delightful book and full of insights and help. Several months ago I could not read it. Now I can.

Grandy says, "Grief always takes longer than anyone wants it too." How true! So settle down and learn what God wants you to learn.

October 20

I'm tired of this valley. I long to get through it and see the light on the other side. I want to be healed. Or do I?? It's scary to think of what may be out there beyond this dark time. At my age, life will possibly never be bountiful again. And I feel that I can never enjoy life again without Wesley. Besides, this valley is becoming familiar. Must I keep on growing after this?

Lord, I submit to Your refining in this valley. I also need courage to face life beyond this grief.

He Bottles Our Tears

Every teardrop, like a snowflake,
Is unique in its own way,
And every one that falls is recorded,
By the One who bottles all our grief—
The One who has experienced,
True sorrow Himself.

Sometimes gushing like a fountain,
Or flowing gently like a stream,
Each tear begs to share its story.

But as the teardrops glisten in the light of the Son,
And fall from each grieving heart,

The Father adds His sweetness,
Until they form a liquid fragrance,
As costly as the most expensive perfume.

One day God will not only wipe away,
Every tear from our eyes.

Perhaps He will also present to us,
The very bottle of tears He has kept,
As a treasure near His heart—
So we can pour it upon His feet—
Our sacrificial offering of praise to Him.
                    - *Rebecca Barlow Jordan*

This precious poem was in a card Fianna gave me.

"Lord, is it true that every tear is saved and recorded? That is too awesome! If so, You have quite a collection of my tears by now. Lord Jesus, will You allow me the privilege of pouring them out on Your feet, as a sweet fragrant sacrifice? Just like Mary. I shed more tears when I think about that. Even now, by faith I give You my tears, as a gift, because I love You and because I sorrow much. I feel badly sometimes, because I can't give You the sacrifice of song and music, but if You will have my tears, I gladly give them to You. . . ."

October 21

I haven't had a sleepless, tear-filled night in; let's see, four or five nights.

Thank you, Lord!

Thank you, Lord!

When you lie down, you will not be afraid.
When you lie down, your sleep will be sweet. (Proverbs 3:24)

October 26 ... the six-month mark.
Pain.
Loneliness.
The pain is less acute.
Loneliness is much heavier.
The Lord is close to the broken hearted. And saves those who are crushed in spirit. (Psalm 34:18-19)

November 2
My Lord, hear this song:
What a day that will be, when my Jesus I shall see ...
When I look upon His face,
The One who saved me by His grace ...
What a day, glorious day that will be!!

Lord, forgive me if this is all wrong:
I want to see Wesley's face too.
I want to feel his warm embrace.
I want to hear his voice.
I want to walk beside him.
Lord, I think You understand.

November 3
Lord, I don't know who I am—now.
Wesley and I were a unit, a complete unit. We were whole, in each other.
We were two halves–
To make a whole.
We were one.
Now the oneness is broken and shattered.

I can run only on half power.
My needle is broken,

My song unaccompanied.
My wheel has no hub.
Who am I Lord?

I was Wesley's other half.
He was my sunshine.
We were together. Now we are separate.

I am like a broken vessel. (Psalm 31:12)
I am as a sparrow—alone—upon the housetop. (Psalm 102:7)
Jesus, Lover of my soul, let me to Thy bosom fly!

November 4

It's twilight, and I step out on the deck. The sunset sky is alive with color and the harvest moon has already bulged, coming to full, and climbing the eastern sky. The Sweet Gum tree is glowing, as though it is lit from within.

A dozen or more birds are chirping their good night song, and fussing, trying to find a comfortable roosting position in our row of hemlocks. Cardinals? A few, but mostly robins! Where did they come from?

It is so beautiful and peaceful, I think I will cry. I do.

November 12

Dear Wesley,

It's Lisa's birthday. I'm remembering 30 some years ago . . . You drove furiously and prayed fervently, all the way to the hospital. God was gracious in sparing me and our baby.

It's good to remember good times. I wonder if you ever think of our family and our years together. I wonder where you are in Eternity . . . past? present? future? Where are you in space? Paradise? Heaven? Highest Heaven? Third Heaven? the Grave?

So many questions. Perhaps none matters. I love you Wesley,

no matter where or when you are. I will love you forever.

- Martha

November 13
I have these old pretzels . . . seven months old? They are good for nothing except for stewing! But guess I'll throw them out.

November 21
Lord, Heaven and Eternity is becoming more obscure and mysterious and very far away and, yes, scary. The realm where Wesley is...whatever and wherever that is—is so completely separate from my existing realm. I find it confusing and dreadful.

Lord, You know my frame; You remember that I am dust. (Psalm 103) *You know how difficult it is for this earthy to think in heavenly concepts.*

November 23
Dear Wesley,

Watch for me. I'll soon be along.

You don't have to draw pictures in the sand while you wait, as the song suggests. I'm so glad you can enjoy all of it now. I'm also so glad you don't have to go through what I'm going through; I wouldn't wish it on anybody!

- Your Martha

December 1
It's been seven months now.

How am I doing?

In a word—plodding. It's very wearisome, just plodding along.

December 10
I don't want to think about it. I try very hard not to think about: My life without Wesley. My widowhood. My future.

Perhaps it will go away.
Perhaps there are no answers.
Perhaps there is no end to this valley.
Perhaps the sun will never shine again.
Perhaps . . .

December 15
Dear Wesley, my Beloved,

Sometime over the Thanksgiving weekend some of the family took me up the hill to your grave. Friends bring gifts to your memorial stone all along—flowers, cards, pictures. This time there was a yellow delicious apple in a glass bowl. Becky brought you two silk arrangements of poinsettias. Anyway, there were piles of brown leaves all around. I raked them together with my hands and piled them on a mound over your bed. I liked the cozy feeling it gave me.

Then I heard them—the robins! A flock of about six robins high in the bare trees, chirping to get my attention. I remembered a song Ralph Stanley sings on a new video I got, "A Robin Built a Nest on Daddy's Grave." I told those robins would they please stay around and build a nest in the Spring. Because . . . roses will bloom again!

Your Dearest Earthy Friend,
- Martha. IGD

December 16
I have peace.
I have hope.
Joy eludes me.

December 17
There is plenty to do:
A house to clean. Letters and cards to write,

Books to read, videos to watch. Plants to water.
Christmas letters to send. Walks to take. Cookies to bake.
Phone calls to make. Tears to shed.

Places to go:
The Nursing Home. The library.
Church. Women's Bible Study.
Rosie's house. Belle's house.

There is plenty to do, so why do I sit here, doing nothing?

December 23

For a number of years it has been a tradition for Wesley to sing, "Mary, Did You Know?" at our annual church Christmas program. Last year he sang it at full power to a teary audience. You see, he had leukemia and wasn't expected to live until Christmas. This year he is gone. There were tears again when son, Steve, and Sarah, with her guitar did, "Mary, Did You Know?" The tradition continues.

Beverly said, "Often, it still seems I can hear Wesley's voice singing, 'Mary, Did You Know?' Could it be he is singing it to her, now?"

December 29

A full Christmas weekend. Just before Dave's family left, Dave questioned me, "After Christmas blues?" Never before had I even considered that concept. I was always ready to get back to a more normal routine—me and Sugar Daddy enjoying the rest of the winter here at the house.

"Yes, Dave, after Christmas blues, big time!"

But a time is coming and has come, when you will be scattered each to his own home. You will leave me all alone. Yet I am not alone—for my Father is with me. (John 16:32)

January 12, 2004

"Lord, if You design for me to remain alone and lonely the rest of my life, I submit.

If You choose to wait to give me Joy until we meet in Heaven, so be it.

If I am destined to continue to be inactive; not 'doing' anything, I accept that.

And if, for reasons I will never know, You will never again in my earthy life, manifest Yourself in a tangible way, if You remain silent in my mortal ear, invisible to my earthy eyes, still I will trust You! Still I will know You are here! Still I know Your promises are being fulfilled, both now and forever! Still I will worship You! Amen."

January 20

Twila took me to Weavertown Church on Sunday morning. Without Wesley.

Memories!

I saw 19-year-old Wes filing into the church house, with his peers, in a long-sleeved white shirt and dark pants, about the middle pew, just across from us girls. Sometimes he stole a glance over our way before he sat down. I could always pick him out, because he sat taller than the rest of the boys.

I remember our day of baptism. There were 15 or 20 of us boys and girls, Wesley included. In turn, Bishop John A. Stoltzfus (Grusdaudy John A.) poured a cup of water on our heads, to baptize us in the Name of the Father, the Son, and the Holy Ghost. On bended knee we confessed that we believed that Jesus Christ is the Son of God and that we would be in obedience to Christ and the Church. All in German. Then Edna Kauffman, Preacher Elam Kauffman's wife, greeted us girls with a holy kiss to welcome us into the fellowship.

I remember many funerals here: my Mother and Father, Sister Anna Mary, Wesley's parents, aunts and uncles, Ben and Mary Lapp's baby.

Our Wedding service: After John A. pronounced us husband and wife, we walked back out the aisle, arm in arm. Wesley gave me the most tender smile. He said later he wanted very much to kiss the bride, but it just wasn't done! That was the beginning of our oneness. Now the tie has been severed.

Through the years, we visited Weavertown Church numerous times. Wesley sometimes preached or gave a testimony. To the "Oldies" he was reminiscent of his grandfather, the revered John A. Stoltzfus. The last time we were here together, he sat in the back with Gerald, I think. Preacher John Lapp asked him to come to the pulpit to testify. Because of his feeble legs, it took him awhile to walk up the aisle. Elsie Kauffman's daughter said, "I was shocked to see Wesley getting old!"

At Weavertown, I wept.

January 27
Call me not Martha, (Naomi).
Call me Marah. . . .
Because the Almighty has made my life bitter.
> Lord, I can't drink this water,
> It's bitter.
> Will You send someone to make it sweet?

I have sent Jesus. He is the Well of Living Water.
Thank you Jesus, for sweetening my bitter water!

* * * *

I have been here with Twila and her family for nearly a month. Now I'm planning to return home. But I dread it. Where is Home?

This "Haven" at Maytown is not home. My house at Slick Rock Hollow . . . the Heart is gone. No place without Wesley is home.

I feel like a homeless person. If "Home is where the heart is," then our Home (mine and Wesley's) is in Heaven. In the mean-

New Moon Over Slick Rock Hollow

time I live in temporary housing, in a refugee camp, as an alien or a migrant worker.

It's time to go back. Back to Bowlings Creek.

January 30

Dear Wesley,

You continue to minister to me through your sermons. Isn't that amazing. Sometimes, in reading scripture, I remember you reading and preaching that portion. I'm reading the Moses account and I see you holding a brick before your eyes, saying, "Here a brick, there a brick, everywhere a brick, brick," speaking of Pharaoh's level of commitment to the Lord. And the scripture in Exodus 3 became more meaningful:

I have indeed seen the misery of Martha. I have heard her crying, I am concerned about her suffering. I have come down to rescue her.

Thank you, Lord.

Thank you, Wesley.

It's in church related activities—worship, singing, scripture—where it's hardest to control my emotions.

I love you Wesley. I always will.

- Your Martha

February 7

At home again, at Slick Rock Hollow, alone. It was very good to be with people the past month. I didn't know if it would help, but it did.

The burden is lighter. I feel better. Thank you, Lord.

Bless their hearts, Phil and Rosie spent the evening with me yesterday. We watched a Blue Grass music video together, and Phil is taking responsibility for my income tax reports. Everyone helps, in their various ways. So good!

February 12

Used to, when I had a bad day, or Wesley was tired and depressed, or we were sick, or there were church concerns—I knew it would get better, either in the morning, or next week, or next spring, things would be better. Now I am chronically sad and will continue to be sad, not forever, but for a long time.

I read a condensed version of the novel *Words by Heart* by Onida Sebestyem, a post-black-slave story. When her husband was murdered, she was a pretty woman, but, "She would never look the way she used to look." Just so—I will never feel the way I used to feel.

February 13

A very good day:

Rosie came and spent several hours.

I walked down to Bessie's old place.

The sun shone all day.

Bev and Rhonda came to visit and to meet Little Rachel Stoltzfus, my new Amish doll. They brought soup and desert and flowers.

Fianna called.

Dave called.

Twila called.

Maxine called.

I typed my Bible story for Fern.

Fern called.

Bo Chandler called.

Cristal Bontrager wrote by email.

Carol Graber wrote by email.

Lael Barkman called.

Many birds at my feeder.

"Thank you, Lord, for friends, who fill my days with warmth and words and comfort. Amen."

February 14

Valentine's Day.

Mike and Connie brought me a bouquet of cut flowers with a heart. Rocky and Rhonda brought a potted rose colored miniature rose. Marcia sent me a valentine card.

"Wesley, I almost thought I would find a card from you lying somewhere around. I didn't find any so I went to my box to find a dozen or more old cards. I found the special one (they are all special!) you gave in 2002. Last year you gave it again, with a tender letter and this message, in a shaky hand, 'X Renewed 02/14/03 with love and commitment W. A.'"

Wesley, I love you more than ever, but how can I let you know?
- Your Sweetheart

February 29

Written from Lisa and Keith's house:

Wesley, as long as we are apart from each other, that's how long my heart will ache. It looks like you aren't coming back, so I will plan to come to you. The only question is: when?

Lisa's new baby is a girl. Her name is Emily Lavonne Miller. Isn't that a pretty name? I think so too.

- Your beloved
Martha. IGD.

March 18

Awhile back I listened to the first CD recording of Wesley's memorial services. Finally today I had the courage to listen to the second CD, Phil's message. It was like I experienced the service all over again, a beautiful eulogy for a great man—the greatest man ever, in my life. Phil recounted the last years and days of Wesley's life, "He finished strong." It was beautiful. Even though I cried all alone, through the whole thing, it was still very beautiful. I need to tell Phil how much I appreciate that.

March 19

It was a beautiful day, so I donned a shirt and gloves, picked up my rake and hoe and "piddled" outside—cleaned flower beds, raked leaves and pine needles, planted peas, watched the birds. After that I felt so much better.

I need to remember that and get out and work more often.

April 2

The last several days have been heavy, weepy. I'm extremely lonely and homesick. Then I tend to forget the good days, when I feel good. There have been those days, but when were they?

So I sing this song again:
> Be still my soul, the Lord is on thy side.
> Bear patiently the cross of grief and pain . . .
> Be still my soul, when change and tears are past,
> All safe and blessed, *we shall meet at last.*

Thank you Jesus!

April 4

Dear Wesley.

The Bradford pear tree is in full bloom. Do you remember last year this time? You are sitting in a lawn chair, under the pear tree with your walker beside you. I am sitting beside you. You are wearing a mask because of spring pollen, but your eyes are smiling. You are watching the Turner boys plow and telling them how! Shirley stopped by and we chatted. You called Rhonda and chatted with her. You were so happy!

I suppose I will remember that, every year when the pear tree blooms. The cherry trees are blooming in D.C. I wonder which trees are blooming on each side of the river of Life where you are. Wish I were there with you!

- Martha. IGD.

April 26

It's been a year.

I need to write about it, to somehow bring closure—not to my grief, I'm not ready to wash and put away my tear soup pot—but to bring closure to this year.

Many things haven't changed since last April. I have the same haunting questions:

> Where, in eternity, is Wesley?
> What, in infinity, is he doing? And does he think about me?
> Will I ever again "enjoy" life?
> Does God have a future for me—here? Now?
> How long? How long? 'Til I reach the end of this valley?
> The Lord God gave Wesley and me a "oneness" in our marriage. Now it is completely severed. Why?

Some things have changed:

My awareness of the care and prayers of many, many friends. I never knew how **very much** people loved and cared.

My deep gratitude for my family. They are awesome! They are "here" for me in so many ways.

Spring is again beautiful!

After a year, the level of crushing pain has lowered. Lonely is still very much with me. I didn't know that loneliness would feel like this.

After a year, I miss Wesley more then ever. During my birthday time and the anniversary of his death and now our 50th wedding anniversary, when so many people offered cards and prayers and calls and kindnesses, subconsciously I expect a phone call from him or a letter, or his car coming down the approach. I know he won't be back but somewhere in the depths of my heart—I wish!

* * * *

Without question, this has been the most difficult year of my life—in every way. If I should decide which area has been one of the most difficult, I would say giving up the role of a preacher's wife (and this surprised me). Being in ministry with Wesley was so rewarding.

Nevertheless . . .

Those haunting questions and dismal observations **do not shake my faith** in an all wise, all loving God and friend who knows exactly what He is doing and why. I don't. From the beginning, and continually, I have **received from Him** this valley of grief. I know He will not abandon me, He will redeem my loneliness, He will complete the work He has begun in me. And I am learning to give back to Him, as a sacrificial gift, my loneliness and pain and tears.

I reaffirm my belief that roses will bloom again, that joy will come in the morning. And just perhaps there is hope for this life, not only for eternity.

There is Hope for today!

There is Hope for next year!

New Moon Over Slick Rock Hollow

Sometimes I feel I'm up against a wall of deep despair,
And I hurt so much that I can't cry.
That's when I say to you,

"Oh, that I had the wings of a dove,
Then I would fly away;
I would rest my head in your quiet wilderness,
And I would not be afraid."

From *Psalm* by Sarah Stoltzfus, granddaughter
And from Psalm 55:7

New Moon Over Slick Rock Hollow